ROAD TRIPPING

ROAD TRIPPING

LORALEE LEAVITT & RICK WALTON

Published by Familius LLC, www.familius.com

Familius books are available at special discounts for bulk purchases for sales promotions, or for family or corporate use. Special editions, including personalized covers, excerpts of existing books, or books with corporate logos, can be created in large quantities for special needs. For more information, contact Premium Sales at 559-876-2170 or email specialmarkets@familius.com

Library of Congress Catalog-in-Publication Data

2013954953

pISBN 978-1-939629-04-3
eISBN 978-1-938301-58-2

Printed in the United States of America

Edited by Emily Smith
Cover Design by David Miles
Book design by Maggie Wickes

10 9 8 7 6 5 4 3 2 1

First Edition

Table of Contents

Introduction

It was Sunday afternoon in one of Glacier National Park's outhouse-but-no-water "primitive" campsites, the only spot left during a crowded Labor Day weekend. We'd spent Saturday exploring the park, hiking up dusty trails, and driving along windy mountain highways. By Sunday, the campsite had emptied out, so it was just our family, with my children playing in the forest and my husband packing up the tent. As I reveled in the quiet, I was struck by a feeling of utter peace, with no electronics, no novels, and no distractions taking me away from my family. The nine-hour drive to Glacier seemed a small price to pay for such a perfect moment.

—Loralee Leavitt

In the fall of 1999, I was working at home as a freelance writer while my wife was being a mom and homeschooling our four children. We had nothing to tie us down. So we decided to take an adventure that admittedly only few families can take and we were only able to take once. For three and a half months we traveled around the country: six people in a minivan for fifteen thousand miles. We saw the leaves change three times—in upstate New York, in Connecticut, and in North Carolina. We slept overnight in a motel made of train cabooses. We survived a hurricane. We saw more museums and historical sites than most people see in a lifetime. That trip created many of our family's favorite memories and led to important learning and bonding. It's not for everyone, but it worked for us.

—Rick Walton

To most parents, long road trips sound like torture. To the authors of this book, long road trips become exciting adventures. Rick's family has traveled all over the United States, including a fifteen-thousand-mile road trip from Utah all along the East Coast. Loralee's family has logged over fifty thousand miles of road trips to Washington, Utah, Colorado, California, South Dakota, Arizona, and Canada. We've packed babies along miles of sandy beaches, cajoled toddlers up forest trails, and urged reluctant children through museums. We've seen incredible natural marvels like Niagara Falls, California's redwoods, Colorado's sand dunes, and Utah's rock arches. We've explored manmade wonders like Mesa Verde, Mount Rushmore, and Hoover Dam. The wonder we felt at each stop was multiplied by our children's reactions as we saw new sights through their eyes.

We've learned how to plan trips, what to pack, and how to save money as we travel. Even more important, we've learned how to keep the journey fun, even when days get long and exhausting.

We've also weathered countless road-trip catastrophes. We've endured screaming children, vomit, dirty diapers, dead car batteries, flat tires on Oregon mountains, Utah blizzards, and forest-fire detours in Colorado. We know how hard it is to pack a car and hit the road. But every time one of our families prepares for a trip, we endure the headaches, the late nights, and the exploding list of labors because we know what's coming: family time we can really enjoy together.

People shake their heads in disbelief and ask, "How do you do it?" The truth is, any family can take a long road trip. All it takes is preparation, time behind the wheel, and determination to keep your family's spirits up, no matter the situation. In this book, we'll share all our tips and tricks, as well as ideas from other experienced travelers, for how you can take a successful road trip—and enjoy it.

CHAPTER ONE

Where Are We Going?

I'd been looking at maps of Utah, Colorado, and South Dakota, because I was jealous that my sister was about to take a road trip to Mount Rushmore. But we'd already scheduled our family trip to go to Utah. Finally, I persuaded my husband that he needed to drive to Denver at the end of our Utah trip to visit his aging grandparents, and once we were there, I showed him the map. "Mount Rushmore's only six hours away," I urged. "It won't add on much time at all!" So we took an extra day, drove up to see Mount Rushmore, and then headed home along beautiful I-90. —Loralee

You're going to pack everybody in the car and drive off on a crazy adventure. But first you have to decide where you're going. How much time do you have? Will you be visiting family? Do you want to introduce your children to the wonders of America's national parks? Or do you prefer theme parks, like Disneyland? Does your family love the outdoors? Big cities? Skiing? Do they like to hang out in hotels and swim? What is their favorite thing to do? What's something new you want to try?

When you're deciding where to go, make it a family decision. Parents should have the majority vote, since it's your schedule, your time behind the wheel, and your money. But you should involve your children as much as possible, because they'll enjoy the trip far more if they get to help plan it.

Here are some things to consider as you plan your trip.

FINANCES

A vacation doesn't have to be expensive. There are a number of ways to travel on the cheap. You can camp, you can stay with people, or you can stay at inexpensive motels. You can sleep overnight in your car in truck stop parking lots. You can buy food in grocery stores and prepare it on your own. You can go to nearby destinations instead of long trips far away.

> On our fifteen-thousand-mile trip across America, we kept costs low by making it a business trip. I did twenty-two days of paid school visits in six states, visited publishers, and researched and wrote books. Much of the trip we were able to write off from our taxes. We kept housing costs down by camping and by staying with friends, relatives, and strangers. We figured out ways to cut other costs—tips you will find in this book. We also took into account the fact that we would be saving money we would normally spend on food, utilities, and other purchases if we had stayed at home. —Rick

COMBINING DESTINATIONS

If you have several places you'd like to visit, can you combine them into one trip? Many families tour the national parks, visiting locations like the Grand Canyon, Mesa Verde, and Arches National Park all in one trip.

VISITING ONE AREA

If you like visiting one city at a time, there are thousands to choose from. In the United States, you might want to enjoy jazz music and southern cooking in New Orleans; visit national landmarks and historical museums in Washington, DC; or see world-class art and giant dinosaur skeletons in Chicago. In Canada, you might enjoy the international feel of Toronto, the fourth largest city in North America; the mountains, ocean, and islands of beautiful Vancouver; or the old city of cosmopolitan Montreal, the largest French city outside of France.

When you're visiting one area, consider staying for several days, a week, or even a few weeks. You'll have time to actually get to know the area. You can take your time visiting attractions such as theme parks, zoos, or museums, and even allow time for kid breaks. You can explore a new city and not spend all your vacation time stuffed in a car.

Our family enjoys getting to know a place. We stayed a week in Williamsburg, two-and-a-half weeks on a farm in upstate New York, a month in Florida, and a month and a half in the San Diego area. Extended stays allow us to get to know an area at our own pace, return to attractions that we like more than we thought we would, and take advantage of unplanned opportunities. And we can get much cheaper weekly motel rates. —Rick

TIME

Knowing how much time you have will help you decide where

you want to go. If you have a week or more, you can go anywhere. You could even drive across the country and back! Think about how much time you want to spend in the car and how long you want to be at your destination (or destinations).

If you only have a day or two, consider a day trip or an overnighter. Many people think they need to go someplace faraway and exotic to have a nice vacation. But you probably have beautiful, wonderful places right at your doorstep, places you haven't seen, places you don't even know about. Learn about them, and when you don't have much time, take shorter trips.

I'd lived in Utah for six years before I got around to visiting Bryce Canyon. As I wandered down canyons and up trails, I passed tourists from the East Coast, Germany, and even Japan. All those years, and I'd been only hours away from an attraction so amazing that people flew in from other countries to see it! —Loralee

REST DAYS

Will you be able to send people back to school or work the day after you return? Or will everybody need a day or two to unpack, clean the house, and catch up on sleep? If your family needs a day to recover, plan it into the schedule.

We spent a long day driving so that we could come home and get the children back in school after our Christmas vacation, and we arrived home at 10:30 p.m. The next morning I woke my children up and got them ready for school, even though they were exhausted. Only two hours later, the school called to say that my overtired kindergartener had thrown up in class, and the teacher suggested I keep him home for a few days. He ended up missing more school than if we'd just let him sleep in that first day home! —Loralee

COMBINING VACATION WITH WORK

Sometimes you can combine a work trip with a family vacation if you have meetings or a conference in a distant location. Combining work with family travel might cover some of your expenses or give you more time when you get where you're going. On the other hand, if you're working during your vacation, you might have less time with your family.

> When I worked selling books, I used to drive from Toronto through Montreal, Quebec City, New Brunswick, and Nova Scotia. It's a pretty spectacular trip. Even better, when I was driving my route I could tack on a quick sightseeing trip to New York, New England, Niagara Falls, Buffalo, or the Adirondacks. —Mark

If you are piggybacking one on the other, see if there are ways your job can add to the vacation experience.

> As a writer who works from home, I was able to involve my kids in my business traveling. My kids would frequently accompany me when I did school presentations. We took tours of my publishing houses, and one of my editors took the family on a tour of the Central Park Zoo. Other editors took us all to lunch in their publishing building. Our kids had a lot of fun, and they got a lot of free books. —Rick

MISSING SCHOOL

If you're planning a trip during school time, consider the pros and cons of taking your kids out of school. How much instruction would they miss? How much homework would they have to make up? Are they struggling with classes that they shouldn't miss? Will your trip be educational? Visiting national parks or historic sites might have a different value than just visiting a theme park when you're hoping it won't be crowded, and those visits might teach children more than a theme park would.

If you decide to pull them out of school for the trip, try to plan in advance with their teachers so that they can get as much work as possible done before they go. Some teachers might even make arrangements for them to do work in conjunction with the trip, because smart teachers recognize that traveling is also educational.

When my daughter's friend was in first grade, her mother took her out of school for five weeks to visit grandparents in New Zealand. She thought the teacher might object, but the teacher was fine with it. —Loralee

If you work from home, or if you homeschool, you'll also have more flexibility to travel. You could even travel for months at a time.

We homeschooled for a few years. Since I work from home, we had absolute flexibility. We traveled for five months straight. We found that we didn't need to follow a strict curriculum while we traveled. The travel itself, if the children were engaged in the trip, was curriculum enough. —Rick

If you have the flexibility, consider visiting busy places during the off-season to avoid crowds. National parks might look very different if you visit in winter instead of summer. Theme parks might be less crowded during the school year.

My best day at Disneyland was a rainy Thursday in February. Since there were no lines, we were able to walk onto all the rides, and Splash Mountain couldn't make us any wetter than we already were. Of course, by the end, we were freezing! —Loralee

We tried to go to see the giant redwoods in Muir Woods, just north of San Francisco, on Thanksgiving Day. The place was packed. We went for a drive instead. The next day we arrived early, before the visitor center opened. We were the first visitors there. For about a half hour we were alone with the giant redwoods. It was magic. Another time, we arrived early at Mesa Verde. We were alone with the Anasazi ruins. More magic. (Of course, we acted respectfully and paid our entrance fees on the way out.) —Rick

SPUR-OF-THE-MOMENT TRIPS

If you have a family emergency, a sudden travel inspiration, or a weekend that opens up unexpectedly, don't be afraid to jump in the car. When the trip is worth it, you can get out the door after only a few hours of preparation. Never turn down an opportunity because you don't think you have the time.

It was 1:30 a.m. one Saturday morning when I learned there would be a rare solar eclipse the next day. The trouble was, the best viewing sites were a thousand miles away. We packed suitcases and travel snacks all morning and hit the road at 4:00 p.m. The following evening, we watched from a remote Utah mountaintop as the moon inched in front of the sun and our shadows fuzzed with crescent shapes. I've never seen anything like it, and I wouldn't have missed it for the world. —Loralee

When you're planning a family trip, don't get overwhelmed by the possible challenges and give up on your plan. If you really want to do it, you can make it happen.

We don't say, "Is this doable?" We say, "This is doable." After all, what am I afraid of? That if I go, one of my kids might get tired or have a fit? So what? They might get tired or have a fit at home. If it's physically doable, you just do it! —Rachel

RESOURCES FOR TRAVELING IN THE UNITED STATES

Books

101 Places You Gotta See Before You're 12! by Joanne O'Sullivan

Road Trip USA: Cross-Country Adventures on America's Two-Lane Highways by Jamie Jensen

Travel Websites

www.fodors.com

www.moon.com

www.tripadvisor.com

www.aaa.com (May redirect you to a local AAA website.)

State Tourism Websites

Alabama: www.alabama.travel

Alaska: http://www.travelalaska.com

Arizona: http://www.arizonaguide.com/

Arkansas: http://www.arkansas.com/

California: www.visitcalifornia.com

Colorado: www.colorado.com

Connecticut: http://www.ctvisit.com/

Delaware: http://www.visitdelaware.com/

Florida: www.visitflorida.com

Georgia: http://www.exploregeorgia.org

Idaho: http://www.visitidaho.org

Illinois: http://www.enjoyillinois.com

Indiana: http://www.in.gov/visitindiana

Iowa: http://www.traveliowa.com

Kansas: http://www.travelks.com

Kentucky: www.kentuckytourism.com

Louisiana: http://www.louisianatravel.com

Maine: www.visitmaine.com

Maryland: http://visitmaryland.org

Massachusetts: http://www.massvacation.com

Michigan: www.michigan.org

Minnesota: http://www.exploreminnesota.com

Mississippi: http://www.visitmississippi.org

Missouri: http://www.visitmo.com/

Montana: www.visitmt.com

Nebraska: http://www.visitnebraska.com

Nevada: www.travelnevada.com

New Hampshire: www.visitnh.gov

New Jersey: http://www.visitnj.org

New Mexico: http://www.newmexico.org

New York: http://iloveny.com

North Carolina: www.visitnc.com

North Dakota: www.ndtourism.com

Ohio: www.discoverohio.com

Oklahoma: www.travelok.com

Oregon: www.traveloregon.com

Pennsylvania: http://www.visitpa.com

Rhode Island: http://www.visitrhodeisland.com/

South Carolina: http://www.discoversouthcarolina.com

South Dakota: www.travelsd.com

Tennessee: www.tnvacation.com

Texas: www.traveltex.com

Utah: www.travel.utah.gov

Vermont: www.vermontvacation.com

Virginia: www.virginia.org

Washington: www.experiencewa.com

West Virginia: www.wvtourism.com

Wisconsin: http://www.travelwisconsin.com

Wyoming: www.wyomingtourism.org

RESOURCES FOR TRAVELING IN CANADA

Books

National Geographic Guide to the National Parks of Canada by National Geographic and Alan Latourelle

Travel Websites

Official Canadian Tourism Site (in English): http://caen-keep-exploring.canada.travel/

National Parks of Canada: http://www.pc.gc.ca/progs/pn-np/index.aspx

Provincial Parks of Canada: http://en.wikipedia.org/wiki/List_of_Canadian_provincial_parks

Ferry Travel (Maine, Massachusetts, Nova Scotia, PEI ferry services): http://www.ferries.ca/fundy-road-trip/?gclid=C-Mjkn5OO8bgCFZFFMgodHU8AvAM

Travel Guide to Visiting Canada (includes useful information for US citizens planning a Canadian trip): http://wikitravel.org/en/Canada

CAA: www.caa.ca

Tourism Websites

Alberta

http://travelalberta.com/ (provincial travel marketing site)

http://www.tpr.alberta.ca/ (Alberta parks)

http://alberta.ca/tourism.cfm (provincial site)

British Columbia

http://www.hellobc.com/ (official tourism and travel website for BC)

http://www.bcferries.com/ (ferries to Victoria/Vancouver Island, Inside Passage islands, and Washington State)

Manitoba

http://www.travelmanitoba.com/ (provincial government marketing site)

http://www.traveltomanitoba.ca/ (Manitoba regional tourism network)

Newfoundland

http://www.newfoundlandlabrador.com/PlanYourTrip/TravelBrochures?gclid=CMrC1euN8bgCFck7MgodrzoAAw (provincial travel marketing site)

New Brunswick

www.tourismnewbrunswick.ca/ (official provincial site)

Nova Scotia

novascotia.com/ (provincial government marketing site)

Ontario

http://www.ontariotravel.net/TCISSegmentsWeb/main.portal?_nfpb=true&_pageLabel=pf_main_pg&language=en (Ontario tourism marketing partnership site)

https://www.facebook.com/OntarioTravel (Ontario tourism on Facebook)

http://www.ontariooutdoor.com/ (Ontario tourism marketing partnership site with an outdoors focus)

Prince Edward Island

www.tourismpei.com/ (official provincial site)

Quebec

http://www.tourisme-montreal.org/ (Montreal municipal site)

http://www.bonjourquebec.com/qc-en/aubaines0.html(official
   provincial tourist site—English link)

www.quebecregion.com/ (Quebec City municipal site)

Saskatchewan

www.sasktourism.com (official provincial site)

Nunavut / Northwest Territory / Yukon Territory

travelyukon.com/ (Yukon Territory official site)

yukonwild.com (a consortium of Yukon travel guides and out-
   fitters serving the whole territory)

www.nunavuttourism.com/ (Nunavut official site)

www.spectacularnwt.com/ (Northwest Territory official site)

CHAPTER TWO

Let's Start Planning

It's a little bit dangerous to plan a trip to someplace new. Once I get online and start reading about all the sights, attractions, museums, and restaurants where we're going, I want to do it all! My husband has to bring me back to earth by pointing out that it's impossible to do everything. So we have to start narrowing down our list to what's important, what my family can handle, and (most important) what we want to pay for.
—Loralee

Once you know where you're going, it's time to decide what to do when you get there. What things must you absolutely see and do? (Keep these to a minimum to have more flexibility.) Is there an event you want to go to? Someone you want to see? Or do you just have a general destination? How will you find attractions that work for your whole family? How much money will you spend? Where will you stay?

ACTIVITIES

Some families like to sightsee on vacation, some like to visit amusement parks, some like to hike, and some like to relax. Whatever your family likes to do, you can tailor your trip to meet your family's needs by gathering ideas ahead of time, researching attractions, checking local event calendars, investigating unusual opportunities, and figuring out how to make your trip fun for everybody.

Getting Ideas

You can start gathering ideas long before you leave on your trip. Read guidebooks and travel guides. Search online for events, museums, and other fun destinations. Take notes and save articles from magazines and newspapers. Ask friends and acquaintances for ideas: you might be surprised to learn who has been to your destination and what tips they can share.

Once you've settled on your destination, take the time to look up local newspapers or websites. This search might lead you to quirky, out-of-the-way destinations that won't show up in national travel guides. Plan to pick up a local newspaper when you arrive to look for other ideas for sightseeing and events, along with dates, times, and prices. You can add these to your list of things to do if you have time. Prioritize everything according to the things that will work the best and the things that you most want to go do.

> I always save travel articles from magazines and newspapers. One article in FamilyFun magazine taught us about gem hunting, which we tried on our next trip. Another tiny article in our local newspaper, about neighbors who complained about noise from a Utah farm, inspired me on our next visit

to Utah. We drove in, left money in the basket to pay for two bags of feed, and fed elk, bison, and a Texas longhorn steer. I would never have heard of this place if I hadn't noticed that article. —Rachel

Involve Your Children

If you invite your children to contribute ideas for your trip, they'll get more excited about it. Ask them what they really want to do and see if you can fit it in. You might give them a list of possible activities to vote on or let them select from a few specific options. You might also research possible places to stop along the way and let them each choose the one they want to see. Also, find out if there's anything else your children want out of your trip. For instance, do they have a favorite hamburger stand or play area where you can stop for a rest break? Such simple pleasures can help keep kids happy when you travel.

On our last drive to Colorado, we let each child choose one thing to do. Kait wanted to try gem hunting, Lauren wanted to go horseback riding, and Alex wanted to swim. So we drove to a sapphire mine in Montana, stopped nearby for horseback riding, and then drove to Colorado where Alex got to swim in Grandma's pool. List accomplished! —Rachel

Planning Your Route

Today's online maps, GPS systems, and smartphone apps make it easy to plot out your routes. As you plan your drive and examine maps, you might see other places you'd love to explore.

On one drive, my husband decided we'd stay at a campground he'd seen on an Idaho map: Bruneau Dunes State Park. In the morning, we hiked up a sand dune overlooking a quiet river, with the sand getting hot beneath our feet. A spot on the map became a wonderful memory. —Loralee

AAA or CAA

If you're a member of AAA (the American Automobile Association) or CAA (the Canadian Automobile Association), visit your local service center for free domestic maps and tour books with ideas for sights to see, as well as suggestions for approved lodging and dining. AAA or CAA will also compile a personal TripTik Travel Planner for you, which includes travel directions for your route. You can even create a TripTik or find printable maps online.

Don't worry about losing your AAA or CAA benefits when you cross the US-Canada border. Whichever membership you hold, you will receive the full range of benefits in either country.

FAMILY-FRIENDLY ACTIVITIES

When planning your activities, consider your children's ages. If you're traveling with very young children, you'll probably want to avoid grown-up events like operas, classical concerts, or art museums. Expecting your children to sit for hours of performance or dragging them around attractions that bore them leads to whining children, frustrated parents, and stares from irritated patrons. You'll also want to avoid long hikes or activities that your children can't do.

Instead, consider activities the children will enjoy, such as Disneyland, parks, zoos, or children's museums. Involving your children in trip planning will help you find out what they're really interested in. Ideally, you'll be able to find activities the whole family can enjoy.

I wasn't excited about visiting the children's museum in Pullman, Washington. But as we explored, I found puzzles to solve, animals to admire, and interactive exhibits that were really fun! My kids and I sent telegraph messages, tossed basketballs while wearing prismatic glasses, and built chutes to roll balls downhill. When it was time to leave, we all wanted to stay longer—especially me! —Loralee

National Parks

North America has some of the most beautiful national parks in the world, as you'll learn when you meet tourists from around the globe. The parks are also terrific destinations for families on a budget, since a family pass lasts for a year and gets you into parks all over the country.

Many families visit several national parks in one trip. For instance, in the American Southwest you might visit Arches, Mesa Verde, and the Grand Canyon, or combine Mount Rushmore and the Badlands when you visit South Dakota. If you visit Banff National Park in Canada, you don't want to miss nearby Jasper National Park.

On our last driving trip, we looped through southern Colorado and Utah. We saw Great Sand Dunes National Park, Mesa Verde, and Arches, all with our national parks pass. As we traveled, we met people from all over the country—grandparents from South Dakota whose car helped us cross another license plate off of our list, a devout Christian family visiting national parks as they journeyed to join a new commune, and even an Amish family that had hired a driver to chauffer them from Ohio. All of them were visiting as many national parks as they could. —Loralee

Find more spectacular destinations at state and provincial parks. For example, you can see wild bison and magnificent granite spires in South Dakota's Custer State Park or see badlands and dinosaur bones at Alberta's Dinosaur Provincial Park.

Museum Memberships

If there's one attraction where you want to spend a lot of time, check the price of an annual family membership. It may be cheaper than paying admission for separate visits, you might get extras like movie tickets, and you'll be able to exit and return whenever you want to give worn-out children a break.

Don't forget to look into reciprocal member admissions. Your membership in a local museum or zoo at home might get you into other museums or zoos for free or for discounted prices. It might even be worth buying one of these memberships ahead of time.

> *When I took my children to a science museum in Pullman, Washington, I learned that they had a reciprocal arrangement with Seattle's Pacific Science Center. Even though I wasn't carrying my Pacific Science Center membership card, they verified my membership with a simple phone call, and my whole family got in for free. —Loralee*

Factory Tours

Wherever you find a factory tour, take it! They can be really interesting for children, especially if the factory makes something the kids are familiar with, like dolls, candy, or cars. The tours are usually free, and the free samples are always a hit (though there are no free samples of cars). Be careful, because the tours usually end at the gift shop—the ultimate sales pitch.

> *On one California trip, I took my kids on the Jelly Belly tour. At the beginning, I wondered if I was crazy—it was a*

forty-five-minute tour, and I was worried the kids would get bored. But it was really set up well for children. There was a walkway that went all the way around the factory floor, so we got to see everything, and we even got to try new Jelly Belly flavors. The kids loved it. —Rachel

Food

When you're planning, don't forget to include your favorite food stops. Whether it's a hamburger stand, a mom-and-pop diner, or a kind of fast food you can't get at home, put it on the itinerary. You'll need food and rest stops anyway, so why not make it something you can all enjoy?

When we travel to Canada, we always stop at Tim Horton's, a Canadian coffee shop. You can find one just about anywhere, even rest stops. My kids love the Timbits, a.k.a. doughnut holes. —Colette

You can also ask the kids for their ideas. It's another way to help them feel included, and once they're in the car, they'll have something else to look forward to.

My kids love Sonic, but we don't have any in Seattle. When we told them we'd stop for burgers at Sonic on our trip, they were all excited and looked forward to it all morning. On the way back, I told them I was going to surprise their dad with a huckleberry milkshake for his birthday. They were so excited to be in on the secret, it got us all the way from Denver to Idaho! —Rachel

ENJOYING ACTIVITIES FOR PARENTS

Plan your vacation with plenty of kid-friendly activities, but don't be afraid to challenge your kids. They might surprise you. A subject that is boring in school can become an adventure on vacation. Kids don't usually have enough experience to realize how rewarding an experience will be if they pass on possibilities that look boring. They would be missing out on activities that could open minds and hearts and create lasting memories.

Besides, you're the parents. If there are activities you really want to do, be creative and search for a way to make them happen.

Museums

Take your kids to all kinds of museums. They will like some more than others, but they will get something from every museum. So will you.

If you're worried about children getting bored in a museum you really want to attend, be creative. Can you swap roles, with one parent tending children outside while the other parent hurries through before you change places? Can you visit the museum while the baby sleeps in the stroller? Can you let your young child play games on a smartphone or bring a favorite toy? Can you find ways to capture your children's interest? Can you find a museum guide designed for kids, or a children's audio guide? If you can keep up a running commentary, ask your children about colors or animals, let them use a museum computer for two minutes while you read signs, or let them push the buttons on an audio guide, you'll all be happy.

You can also find out whether a museum or similar attraction offers in-and-out privileges. Giving children an outside break and a snack could allow your family another few minutes of precious sightseeing time. At museums with landscaping between buildings, such as California's J. Paul Getty Museum, you can pop into one exhibit and then give your children a break outside before attempting the next.

Performances

If you wish to attend a performance, check your options. Some organizations, such as the Cedar City Shakespeare Festival, provide child care during performances. Other theaters have soundproof rooms where families can watch the show without worrying that their children's noise will disrupt the performance. Some theater companies even offer an occasional show geared towards families, with shorter, kid-friendly performances. If you're staying with family, they might be able to watch children for you, or you could offer to exchange child care with your hosts so that they can have their own evening out.

You'll also have more success with your children if you prepare them ahead of time. If you plan to visit art museums, talk about the paintings ahead of time or learn stories about the artists. Your kids will have a much better visit if you can point out paintings they already know or insert facts like, "That's by the artist who cut off his ear!"

> *When we planned to visit my favorite cathedral, I started telling my daughter about it months before we left. I showed her pictures, told her stories about the building, and taught her the names of all the prominent features. When we walked in, she pointed straight ahead and named the stained glass window. Because she recognized the building, she felt right at home, and we were able to spend a long visit walking around, admiring the features, and pointing out our favorite parts to her. —Loralee*

When you attempt to sightsee with young children, be realistic. You may only see a small portion of a museum or spend only a few minutes at a site where you wanted to linger. Realize that although you'll spend less time sightseeing and more time caring for children than you'd hoped, you can still enjoy yourselves. Seeing these attractions through your children's eyes will give you a new perspective, and you can enjoy your time together.

When we took our children to an exhibit of illustrated medieval manuscripts, my husband kindly took the children so that I could enjoy the exhibit in peace and quiet. Still, I found myself rushing back to my family so that I could show my daughter the paintings of medieval dresses or drag my four-year-old son over to the picture of two monks fishing in a rowboat. Those memories are even more precious to me because I was able to share them with my children.
—Loralee

If you realize your young children will prevent you from visiting your favorite attractions, feel free to postpone that particular trip. The museums, attractions, shows, and parks will still be there in a few years, when you can take your children or travel without them. (On the other hand, if there's a temporary exhibit you can't bear to pass up, use the above tips and go for it!)

LODGING

Where will you stay on your road trip? Does your family prefer hotels, camping, or something else? What does your budget allow?

Whatever lodging you choose, planning ahead will help you cut down on travel costs. You will also be able to find ways to make overnights part of your family adventure.

Hotels

For children, staying in a hotel can be an exotic experience. There might be a swimming pool, cupboards to open, or fancy breakfast food. Many hotels offer portable cribs and other features for families with young children.

Think about the type of lodging that works best for your family. Hotels with interior corridors might provide more safety, but hotel rooms with exterior doors might have fresh air and ventilation. Motel rooms with exterior doors are also closer to your car if you have to haul tired kids or if there are no luggage carts. If mold is an issue, avoid the older, cheaper motels. If industrial chemical odors affect you, the paint and fresh-carpet smells of new facilities might be a problem.

If you plan to stay at a hotel or lodge, do your research ahead of time. You'll be able to compare prices, take advantage of special offers, and ensure you have a place to stay even during busy seasons. You can also find out which hotels offer the features you want, such as breakfast, a swimming pool, or adjoining bedrooms. Always ask about AAA, CAA, entertainment coupons, military, or other discounts you might qualify for. Check TripAdvisor (wwwtripadvisor.com) or Google (www.google.com) for recommendations.

Hotels are expensive, and you don't want to pay more than you need to. Often, you'll get a good price simply by booking your hotel room ahead of time for the prepaid price. Check online to see if you can find a better deal. Occasionally, Hotels.com can offer a lower price because they've gotten a discount by buying blocks of rooms. Alternatively, you can use a website like Hotwire.com. Be aware that Hotwire doesn't allow you to choose a specific hotel by name but instead will find the cheapest place that matches your specifications.

Scheduling

When planning a hotel stay, allow for extra time both in the evening and morning. Children can get so excited about staying someplace new that they won't go to sleep for hours! Also, plan extra time if you're going to take your kids swimming or use any other hotel features.

Airbnb

If you don't want to cram your family into one expensive hotel room, or you'd like a kitchen to save on the expense of eating out, check for rooms and apartments on Airbnb.com. This website helps you search for private rentals in any location and connects you directly with their owners. With room descriptions, photos, and feedback from previous renters, you'll be able to decide if any of the possibilities work for your family. Airbnb rentals may also be cheaper than comparable hotels.

> When we visited Washington DC, the cheapest hotel rooms we could find were well over two hundred dollars a night. Instead, we found an apartment through Airbnb in the exact location we needed, and it saved us money besides! —Loralee

Camping

Another way to save money on lodging is to camp outdoors. Most national and state parks offer campsites that allow you to stay where you're sightseeing. Make sure you do your homework. You may need to reserve such a campsite months in advance, especially if you'd like to use a structure such as a yurt or a teepee. Don't take the chance of finding the campsites full when you get there! Also, check the regulations for specific campsites. You don't want to plan Dutch oven dinners for campsites that have banned campfires or pack lots of unprotected food into bear country.

If camping inside a national park is too difficult, consider possibilities just outside the park. We love Yellowstone. Yellowstone has great campgrounds, but when we went, they were mostly first come, first served, and they filled up quickly. We would stay in a campground just outside the park on the first night and then early in the morning drive in to our chosen campground and cruise until we found an open site. We have also stayed at much cheaper and much more easily available motels just outside the park. —Rick

If you're traveling for several days, don't limit your camping to your destination spot. You may be able to find places to camp along the way, such as a state park, a KOA site, or US Forest Service land. Google Maps (maps.google.com) lists some private campsites, but Google Earth (earth.google.com) is even better, because it lists many state campsites as well.

When we visited Glacier National Park, we packed our food ahead of time, drove there in one day, camped for three days, and drove home. The trip only cost us three hundred dollars, and most of that was for gas money. —Loralee

Staying with Friends and Family

One reason to travel is to spend time with family and friends. Do you have relatives or friends who would be willing to host you? Instead of just dropping in to say "hi," consider staying with them. You'll save money, and you'll strengthen ties—that is, if you're considerate houseguests.

Ben Franklin warned that "Fish and visitors stink in three days." However, three days might not be enough to really have a good time at a location or to enjoy visiting with somebody you don't see often. With careful planning, and consideration for your hosts, you can make your visit a pleasant experience for both parties.

When asking friends and family whether you can stay, plan ahead and give them as much advance notice as you can. Be sensitive to their replies. Does a reluctant "yes" really mean "no"? Do they have scheduling conflicts you need to work around? If they can't host you for several days in a row, can you split your time between two households or stay for a few days and then vacate to a hotel? You don't want to ruin relationships by asking too much.

When you plan to stay with hosts, make sure your children know ahead of time it's not a hotel. They shouldn't expect to be waited on, served, or taken care of. You and your family should make it as easy as possible for family members or friends to host you. Keep your things cleaned up, prepare meals, do the dishes, or help out in any way possible. If you have dietary restrictions, consider buying your own food or doing your own cooking.

You should not spare any expense when staying with friends and family. Remember, you're saving money you would have spent on a hotel. Use that money to support your hosts in whatever way will make your visit easier. Buy food, take the family out to dinner, or pay for admissions to parks and other places. You want to enjoy your time together, support your hosts as they support you, and part as friends!

Last-Minute Travel

Even if you're making a last-minute change or leaving on a spur-of-the-moment trip, you can find travel deals. Use a smartphone or call friends at home to get phone numbers of hotels in the city you want to stop at. Call several hotels so that you can compare prices, ask how big the rooms are, or find out who has cribs and other necessities. You'll be able to find the best room at the best price, instead of settling for the first hotel you stop at.

If you pull in late at night and you know the hotel is not overbooked, be bold and ask for the AAA or CAA rate even if you're not a member. By that time of night, the hotel clerk wants to fill rooms and can likely make a deal.

Alternatively, you might need to call people on the spur of the moment and say, "Hi, we're in town. Can we stay with you?" Do this only with people who you're sure will want you to come and stay.

HOW MUCH TO PLAN

Rick's tip: Do not overschedule. You do not have to see everything in one trip. Vacations aren't about places or things; they are about people. What is going to be the best experience for your family? Rushing, rushing, rushing here and there and trying to keep up with a tight schedule is not conducive to happy family traveling. Give yourself time to breathe. Leave wiggle room for surprises, emergencies, or diversions. Or just stop and rest because you are tired. You can always put in more if you plan well. But don't commit to a rigorous schedule, or you will probably pay for it.

Loralee's tip: Don't overschedule, but do allow for extra sightseeing. Be flexible. Research what's in the area so that if you have extra time, you'll know where to go. Then, if you have time and your kids are up for it, go see one more thing, because you may never come back.

CHAPTER THREE

Preparing to Leave

One Thanksgiving weekend, a policeman knocked on our door. He was wondering if we knew anything about our neighbor, who hadn't been seen for a week. A friend had started to worry and contacted the police. The next Monday, the neighbor was back home—having spent the week vacationing in Canada without telling his friends.
—*Loralee*

When you're preparing to leave home, there are lots of things to take care of. Have you made arrangements for somebody to take care of your yard, pet, houseplants, or newspapers? Is your car ready to go? Are there bills that must be paid before you return? Have you told friends and family about your plans? Is there anything else that will need attention while you're gone?

YOUR HOME

Even though you're leaving your home for a while, you want your home watched and cared for while you're gone. What needs to be done?

Outside

Will you need somebody to water the lawn? Take garbage cans to the street or back to the house? Pull weeds? Take care of pets?

Inside

Think also about the things inside your house. Do you need somebody to water houseplants or feed pets? Do you need to send your pets to other caretakers while you're gone?

A Caretaker

Even if you don't need somebody to take care of your home, ask a neighbor, friend, or family member to watch your home. Make sure this person has a key, as well as your contact information. They should also know who is coming and going from your home, such as the neighbor boy caring for your pets. Also, consider calling your local police department. If your police department has a Vacation House Watch Program, you can request that police officers drive by your house occasionally while you're gone.

A Live-In Caretaker

If you'll be gone for an extended period of time, consider asking somebody trustworthy to stay in your home. You may also want to hire somebody to mow the lawn and do other yard work to keep the yard from getting overgrown and signaling your absence.

Home Security

Police departments recommend several measures to help deter thieves while you're away. One idea is to install at least two light timers that will turn lights on and off in a logical sequence while you're away. Another is to leave a TV or radio playing, or to turn them on and off with a timer.

YOUR CAR

Since you're going on a road trip, you want to make sure your car can carry your family safely. Is the car ready to go? Are you prepared for emergencies?

Regular Maintenance

Before you travel, take care of any regular car maintenance. Get your oil changed, have the tires checked, and get your windshield replaced if it's too cracked to see through. Check to make sure your driver's license, vehicle registration, plates, and car insurance are current, and make early payments on anything that's due during your trip so that nothing expires while you're traveling.

Mechanic Check

You should also take your car in for a thorough checkup with a trustworthy mechanic. Make sure everything is in good working order and that nothing is ready to break down. The last thing you want is to break down by the side of the road, a thousand miles from home.

AAA or CAA

Since accidents happen, despite the very best preparations, consider joining AAA (in the USA) or CAA (in Canada). You'll receive emergency services such as towing, battery service, lockout, flat tire, winching and extrication, and fuel. You'll also be able to order maps and travel e-books to help you plan. Besides emergency assistance, AAA and CAA provide discounts at many hotels, restaurants, and tourist attractions, so you'll benefit from membership even if you don't need roadside assistance.

> *We got our money's worth out of AAA. This service is like insurance or taxes—you benefit if they make money off of you. (If your insurance company makes money off you, that means that you are healthy. If you make money off them, that means that you are having physical problems.) The same is true with AAA. If all goes well, you won't need them at all. But if you're ever stranded on a deserted highway with a dead battery, a flat tire, a locked car, or an empty gas tank, or if you're in an accident, your membership will quickly pay for itself. —Rick*

PAPERWORK

Take care of bills, calendar appointments, and other emergency planning before you go. The last thing you want to realize a thousand miles away from home is that you forgot to pay the phone bill!

Mail and Newspaper

Make arrangements to stop your mail and any newspapers you receive. You don't want mail piling up in your mailbox or newspapers scattered on your porch to alert burglars of your absence. If you can't put these on hold, ask a trusted neighbor to collect your mail and newspapers.

Milk and Groceries

If you have regular deliveries of anything such as milk or groceries, cancel all deliveries for the time you'll be gone.

Calendar

Check to see if you have scheduled anything for the time that you'll be gone, such as doctor's appointments, music lessons, or sports practices. Some professions will charge you for missed visits.

Make sure you've taken care of your responsibilities for when you're gone. You may need to report your plans to your work, volunteer organizations, parent groups, or anybody else who might be counting on you. You may also need to find substitutes to cover for you while you're away.

Bills

Check on any bills that are due soon or will have to be paid while you're gone, including bills for doctors, utilities, kid activities, or anything else. You can pay these early, or use your bank's online bill-pay feature to schedule payments when they're due.

Cell Phone

Find out what charges you'll incur as you travel, especially if you plan on crossing the border. Even if you don't actually leave the country, you might be charged international fees if you place calls while you're close to a border. Check your data plan as well. Downloading can get expensive, especially if you use data in a foreign country. You may want to disable calling or downloading on devices your children use so they don't incur roaming or data charges.

When we traveled to Canada, we called my parents just before we crossed the border so that we wouldn't get charged an international rate. When our phone bill arrived, we found we'd been charged two hundred dollars for an international call, because we were so close to Canada that the call appeared to come from there. It took us hours to straighten out the mess and have the charge removed. —Loralee

It's also easy for a young child to accidentally purchase something online, because many free apps have links to buy other games and will charge you for following those links. Contact your phone company so that they can put a block on your phone, and carefully review the games you let your children play.

I thought the free version of Tetris on my phone was innocent enough, until my three-year-old accidentally followed a link that led to a new game. My next phone bill listed an extra ten-dollar charge. Luckily, the phone company refunded the money immediately and put on a block so that it couldn't happen again. —Loralee

Credit Card
Make sure your credit card is paid off so that you'll be able to use it as you travel. You should also contact your credit card company ahead of time and alert them to your upcoming trip, because many companies will block a card that shows unusual charges, such as charges far from home.

Health Insurance
Make sure you have your health insurance information, including emergency phone numbers. Check your health insurance policy to make sure you'll be covered in the states you'll be visiting.

Emergency Contact Information

Have you told family, friends, and close neighbors where you are going so that they can keep an eye on your home or contact you in case of an emergency? Do you know how to contact them? Cell phones are lifesavers in this day of easy communication, but you can't always count on them. You might lose your phone, run out of battery power, or lose phone reception (a common occurrence on cross-country trips, especially in wilderness areas). Consider giving at least one friend or family member your detailed itinerary, with hotel locations and phone numbers, or alternate ways of contacting you. Let these people know when you plan to be back.

> *My parents send their itinerary out to family members when they travel. It's a good thing, because on one family trip to Costa Rica, my uncle called their hotel with the news that my grandmother had passed away. They were able to keep in touch with family and learn about funeral plans, all because they'd provided contact information ahead of time. —Loralee*

Extra Paperwork

Check to see if there's any other paperwork you need to help you reach your destination. For instance, if you're an American visiting Canada, you may need passports, children's birth certificates, proof of adequate car insurance, an itinerary, or names and addresses of hotels you plan to stay at.

Social Media

Avoid posting your travel plans publicly on the Internet. You may accidentally alert villains that you will be away from home and invite burglary or other problems. If you have older children who use the Internet, ask them also to keep your family plans private. They can post pictures, updates, and travel sagas after you're all back home.

PREPARING IDENTIFICATION

No matter how careful you are, there's always the risk of losing valuables when you travel. Prepare ways to identify your possessions ahead of time, in case they're misplaced or stolen. Even more important, prepare identification for your children in case you get separated.

Label Everything

To keep from losing items, label everything. Take pictures so that you can identify your belongings or show the pictures to someone who might recognize them or know what happened to them. Make a record of serial numbers in case you have to report something as stolen. Beware of labeling your items with your personal information, except perhaps your name and your phone number. Addresses and other personal information might lead undesirable strangers to you.

ID for Children

Make sure that your children have your contact information in case they get lost. Help them memorize phone numbers, especially the numbers for the cell phones you'll be carrying. You might write their phone numbers in coats, on the inside of shoes (some police departments supply in-shoe stickers for this purpose), on rubber bracelets, or on shoelace tags. Consider getting each child an ID of some sort, such as an ID bracelet or lanyard necklace with contact and emergency information, including medical alerts. This is especially important if your child has an allergy or medical condition.

You might also want to make up an ID card, kit, or app to carry with you. If you get separated from your child, you'll have something to show to the authorities so that they know whom to look for.

If you can clear your calendar, pay your bills, check your car, and prepare your children for the trip, you'll have a much easier time when you travel. Instead of worrying about things back home, you'll actually be able to enjoy your vacation!

TRAVEL PREPARATION CHECKLIST

Get Help for Home Care

- Water the lawn.
- Do yard care.
- Move garbage cans.
- Water houseplants.
- Care for pets.
- Watch home.

Car

- Have your car checked.
- Consider joining AAA or CAA.

Paperwork

- Stop mail and newspapers.
- Stop additional deliveries, such as groceries.
- Cancel calendar appointments during trip.
- Take care of responsibilities: report plans and find substitutes.
- Pay approaching bills.
- Pay credit card and alert company to travel plans.
- Check that health insurance will cover travel.
- Share emergency contact information with family and friends.

Identification

- Make records of your personal possessions.
- Consider labeling possessions with some contact information.
- Help children memorize phone numbers.
- Get ID for children.

CHAPTER FOUR

Packing Right

*My friend Lisa packed all her kids' stuff in bins. Even when
her kids were home, she always had basics ready in the bins,
like a toothbrush, underwear, a swimsuit, and a change of
clothing for whatever season. This made packing for trips fast
and easy. She also liked the way it cubed everything in the car.
I asked her about the difficulty of carrying bins into a hotel,
but she said it was never a problem since the kids all carried
their own. —Michele*

Packing is a huge job. You know you need clothes, toiletries,
and emergency supplies. You might need hot weather gear or
cold weather gear, or you might need games and supplies for
your vacation destination. How are you going to pack it and fit
it all into the car?

If you break your packing down into manageable sections,
you'll be able to prioritize and accomplish your tasks one at
a time. Make checklists for your various tasks (see lists at the
back of this chapter).

PACKING LIGHT

You only have so much room in a car. For every item you decide to pack, ask yourself these questions: Will you need it? Is it a necessity, or is it a minor convenience? Is it something you'll find at your hotel, like soap or a hair dryer? If you end up needing it, could you buy it on your trip?

On the other hand, don't skimp on necessities, and don't forget to buy things you might not be able to buy on your trip. If you're camping in the backwoods, you probably won't be able to buy mosquito repellant. If you run out of diapers, you'll have to buy replacements at gas station prices. Travel light if you can, but be prepared for what you need.

INVOLVING KIDS

If your children want to help pack, let them! Help them come up with their own list of things to pack, and let them do as much of it as they can. Check the bags yourself to make sure that they didn't pack six pairs of shoes and no underwear.

When my eight-year-old son packed his suitcase, I gave him a checklist, reminded him what he needed, and checked to make sure he had all the right clothes. Only when we arrived at our destination did we realize he hadn't packed any shoes or hiking boots! That weekend, whether he was playing at the park, hiking to the beach, or going to church, he had to do it in flip-flops. —Loralee

Older children should be able to help with other packing tasks, such as assembling snacks, toys, or coats, or helping younger siblings. If you give them assignments and checklists, and explain how important their jobs are, many children will rise to the occasion and get to work.

You may want to label your children's suitcases with nametags. This will help them pack their things in the right place, and it'll also help you match kids with their luggage when you reach your destination.

WHAT TO BRING

Whether you're traveling to a winter cabin or a summer amusement park, your packing list will include clothing, toiletries, and appropriate child gear. You should also consider what you'll need in the car, what you'll need at your destination, and what you'll need in emergencies.

Clothes

Every person needs clothing. What are you going to bring? For each planned day of travel, pack one set of underwear, a pair of socks, and a shirt, plus an extra of each in case something gets wet or dirty. Pack pants for whatever activities you'll be doing, whether hiking, biking, or sightseeing. Pack more clothes for younger children, who are likely to go through more outfits. Don't forget nice outfits if you plan to go to church or to formal events.

You'll also need pajamas. Plan for the weather, but remember that even in hot weather you might need warm pajamas if you're sleeping in air-conditioned rooms.

To pack light, find outfits that are multipurpose, such as nice button shirts that can be casual or formal. Look for clothes that pack tight, such as nylon shirts that compress more than cotton. A windbreaker and a light jacket take less space than a puffy winter coat, and they make a combination that can withstand almost any weather.

You can bring less clothing if you plan to do laundry on the way. Consider visiting a Laundromat, or ask your hosts whether you can use the washing machine.

Shoes

Bring the shoes that you'll need for your planned activities, whether hiking shoes, walking shoes, formal shoes, water shoes, or beach sandals. Look for multipurpose shoes, such as Chacos for hiking or for the beach, or walking shoes like Mary Janes that you can wear formally. Don't forget easy slip-on shoes for car travel, because you'll want to quickly shove kids' feet into their shoes at gas stations or rest stops.

Toiletries

You'll need toothbrushes for every person, as well as sunscreen, deodorant, shampoo, makeup, hairbrushes, and hair accessories for whoever needs them. Don't forget your hair dryer, unless there will be one where you're staying. Think about the things you use every day and bring what you need.

Medicines

Don't forget the daily dosages of whatever medicines your family members require. Make sure you have plenty for the trip. You may want to stow medicines in more than one place, since you don't want to lose all of your expensive and necessary medication in one misplaced suitcase. Be sure to bring a prescription or your doctor's contact information, in case you need a refill.

You'll also want to bring whatever you need for emergencies, such as allergy medicine or asthma inhalers.

Packing for the Weather

If you're traveling in hot weather, pack appropriately. Remember hats, sunscreen, sandals, and anything else you might need.

If you're traveling in cold weather, make sure that everybody has warm coats, hats, mittens, and whatever else you might need. Try winter gear on children ahead of time, because you don't want to reach the snow and realize that everybody's grown out of their snow boots.

No matter the weather, pack swimsuits. If you end up in a hotel with a swimming pool, you'll be ready.

Laundry Bag

Bring an empty laundry bag for dirty clothes. You'll be able to collect everybody's laundry in one place, and if you have a chance to wash clothes, you'll be ready.

Overnight Bag

If you're arriving at your destination late at night, you won't want your children running wild while you haul in every suitcase and rummage for pajamas. Instead, pack an extra overnight bag with everybody's pajamas and toothbrushes. If you'll be traveling again the next day, add clean shirts and underwear to help everybody get out the door in the morning. Bag each person's clothing in a gallon zip bag. With all the pajamas ready to go, you'll be able to get your children quickly into bed. You can bring in the other suitcases later, or leave them in the car.

Baby Gear

If you're traveling with a baby, make sure you take what you need. Do you need to bring a portable crib, or will there be one at your destination? Do you need to buy diapers or formula before you leave? Did you remember pumps, bottle sterilizers, and any other assorted paraphernalia?

Stroller

If you have young children and room in your vehicle, you'll want a stroller. Not only can you give kids a ride but you'll have a place to stow all your extra gear, like diaper bags, lunches, or coats.

Make sure the stroller has

- Compact size (a two-seat stroller with side-by-side seats might be too wide to maneuver through crowds or tight spaces).
- A seat that reclines to a flat position. If you have a two-seat stroller, you can lower the back seat and allow one child to nap while the second child sits up front. If you have two young children who can (and should) walk most of the time, you can lay down both seats, letting one child sleep in comfort while the other walks.
- Lots of storage underneath for baby supplies, personal items, souvenirs, jackets, and anything you would rather push than carry. The seat itself, with the back lowered, might be the perfect size for a picnic cooler. Strollers are also great for carrying luggage or trundling groceries.
- Lots of nooks and crannies by the handles to keep water bottles, keys, tickets, snacks, baby toys, or anything else you want to have quick access to.
- Easy-lock wheels so that the stroller won't roll away. Large wheels are nice for traversing rough terrain.
- A canopy to shield kids from sun or rain.

Electronics

Look for smartphone apps to help you with your trip. There's an app for just about everything travel-related, such as finding the cheapest gas stations (GasBuddy), checking the lines for crossing the US-Canada border (Border Buddy), or looking up wait times at Disneyland (Mousewait).

Pack your camera, because you'll want good memories of your trip. If you have several to choose from, think about what you need. Will you be taking high-resolution pictures of scenery? Will you be taking videos? Will you need a light, portable camera for hiking? Will you need a kid-friendly camera for your children to use? Or will you just take pictures with your smartphone? Choose the camera that best fits your needs, and don't forget other equipment, like a tripod or extra memory cards.

Whether you're bringing laptops, touchpads, cell phones, cameras, or other gadgets, remember to pack the appropriate chargers and batteries. You'll want to charge the electronics every night to make sure they're always ready to use. Look into options for a car charger or car adapter if you don't have one.

Stow all electronics in a portable bag so that you can carry them with you when you stop for breaks or for the night. You don't want to leave your expensive electronics in the car for thieves.

Supplies for Keeping the Car Clean

A small whisk broom and dustpan are useful for cleanup when crumbs get dropped or dirt gets tracked in. Store the broom and dustpan in the front door of the car or under a seat.

Ziploc bags are great for storing food, toys, wet or dirty clothing, and other odds and ends. They make organizing easy, since you can see what's inside. Have several sizes, from snack to gallon. You'll use them all.

Pack paper towels and baby wipes for spills and sticky fingers. Make sure you have a place to stow garbage, even if it's a simple plastic bag.

PACKING FOR EMERGENCIES

Make sure that you have your spare tire handy and that you know how to change a tire. If you'll be traveling in cold weather, pack chains and a shovel for snow trouble. (You may want to practice using these beforehand, because squatting in the dark by the side of a busy freeway is not the best place to learn.) Bring extra coats and blankets to keep everybody warm in case you have to stop for any reason.

If you've joined AAA or CAA, keep your membership card handy in case you need to make an emergency call.

Extra Car Keys

You never want to lock your only set of keys in the car, especially if you're far from civilization. Make sure that every driver has a copy of your car keys. If you have only one driver, consider having an older child keep an extra set of keys in a zippered pocket. You might also want to hide extra keys in a magnetized key compartment under your car. (Members of AAA or CAA can also call for lock-out assistance.)

Money

Bring cash, checks, and credit cards, because different businesses accept different forms of payment. You'll also want to have coins accessible for tolls or parking meters. Don't keep all the money in one place, because you want to have a backup in case it gets stolen. Be sure you also have extra money for emergencies such as car trouble.

If you're crossing the border, think about how you want to handle foreign currency. Will you get traveler's checks or currency from your bank ahead of time, or will you rely on ATMs and credit cards after you cross the border? Research exchange rates, ATM fees, and international transaction costs to help you decide on the best forms of payment. And be sure to alert your credit card company that you'll be traveling so you don't get stranded with no way to pay.

When we visit Canada, we use credit cards most of the time. But we get some cash as soon as we can, because some of the businesses in my parents' small Alberta town don't accept credit cards. —Colette

Legal Documents

Bring birth certificates, medical prescriptions, and anything else that might identify who you are in case of an emergency. Even if you don't plan on leaving the country, it's not a bad idea to bring your passports. You never know when you may be traveling near the border and decide to take a jaunt into Canada or Mexico.

When the Olympics came to Vancouver, Canada, my husband and I went to an ice skating event. Two weeks later we persuaded my parents that they should go too, but last-minute maneuvering meant that I had to buy their tickets through my own account. To avoid ticketing problems, my husband and I drove up to collect the tickets in person and then showed our children around the Olympic sites. Good thing we all had our proper passports and documentation! —Loralee

Activities for Your Destination

Don't forget to pack the supplies you'll need at your destination, whether it's camping gear, ski equipment, or beach shovels and pails.

If you'll be staying in one place, such as a cabin, consider bringing games and toys, such as board games, puzzles, or movies. Outside toys can be fun and simple things like bubbles, Frisbees, and sidewalk chalk.

GIFT FOR YOUR HOST

If you'll be staying with friends or relatives, consider bringing a thank-you gift. This might be something special from your own family, a regional treat that's local to your area, or something specific to your hosts.

PACKING IT ALL IN

Once you've packed everything, you have to figure out how to get it all in the car.

Put It Where You Need It

When you're packing, consider what you'll need to use during the trip, and pack it where you can reach it. Snacks should be easily available, as should toys, audiobooks, jackets, diapers, and an overnight bag for when you stop.

> I always keep sunscreen and insect repellent in the driver's side door so I don't have to dig for it when we stop for a hike or head to the beach. I can also grab the sunscreen while en route and have the kids pass it around so we are ready when we jump out of the car. (We don't pass the insect repellent around in the car.) —Michele

Using Extra Space

Take advantage of any extra space inside your car. Pack small suitcases, cameras, or flat boxes under seats, or set a cup of pencils in an empty cup holder. You can also stow extra luggage on unused seats or on the floor in front of children with short legs. (Be careful what you put on the floor—you don't want your children's shoes shedding dirt into an open snack box!)

Filling the car might actually become an advantage as you pack luggage around your children in ways to make them more comfortable. For instance, a child might be more comfortable leaning against a soft suitcase than a hard window.

My young sons like to sleep on car trips, so we try to make them as comfortable as we can. We put sleeping bags or suitcases under their feet so their legs aren't dangling, and that gives us more room to store gear. —Amanda M.

Consolidate

If you have little odds and ends, pack them together in boxes and bags. You might have a bag for camera gear, a box for family board games, or a box for food. Choose sizes that fit well in your car.

CAR TOP CARRIERS

If you can't fit everything inside your car, consider using a top carrier. They're inconvenient, and they lower your gas mileage, but they might make it possible for you to travel in comfort. On a long trip, that comfort may be worth the extra gas.

Having a car top carrier also makes it much easier to find your lost car in a large parking lot (and if you use two carriers, you will never lose your car).

If you do go the car top route, there are some things to consider:

- Your carrier might make your car too tall for many parking garages.

- Make sure your carrier shuts securely so that your luggage won't get soaked in a heavy rainstorm.
- Make sure your carrier *cannot fall off.* Don't just trust the factory-provided grips. Consider tying ropes around the tops of the car rack and through permanent fixtures of the car.
- Make sure the lid won't come off. Although rare, this can happen, especially if the wind hits a weak lid at the right angle and with just the right force. Use ropes or bungee cords to fasten the carrier tight.
- With all that security, it would take a very determined thief to rifle through your stuff, but just to make sure, you may want to lock the carrier with combination locks. Locks can also keep the top of a tightly packed carrier firmly fastened and help prevent rain from entering. Otherwise, a tightly packed carrier might bulge, allowing a gap to develop between the edges.
- Don't keep anything valuable, such as money, electronics, or cameras, in your car top carrier, no matter how tightly you've secured it.
- Use the car top carrier for lighter items, such as jackets or sleeping bags, so that you don't injure yourself hoisting anything heavy. Heavy items, such as coolers, can more safely be packed in the car.
- If you need anything for nightly stops, pack it in the car instead of the car top carrier (packing and unpacking a car top carrier is too big a job to do daily). Use the car top carrier for what you'll need at your major destination, such as luggage, sleeping bags, camping gear, or bulky baby equipment.

- If you are a serious car topper, you may want to take a collapsible stepladder so that you can get stuff in and out without risking your life.

We bought a roof rack car top carrier for our latest camping trip and really enjoyed it. Putting the sleeping bags and camping supplies in the carrier gave us extra space to spread out and be comfortable inside our minivan. After we got back, we decided to drive through a car wash. Suddenly, I saw the height restriction sign, remembered that the carrier was still on the car, and yelled, "Stop!" We backed out of the car wash and realized we'd better take the carrier off whenever we were just driving around town. —Colette

You may be wondering how a car top carrier would EVER be worth the bother. All I can say is, with six in a minivan, and later, seven in a Suburban, it saved our lives. —Rick

SAMPLE PACKING CHECKLISTS

Clothes

- Shirts
- Pants
- Socks
- Underwear
- PJs
- Outdoor clothes
- Outdoor shoes
- Formal clothes
- Formal shoes
- Raincoat
- Warm coat
- Snow clothes
- Swimsuit
- Sandals
- Hats

Toiletries

- Tooth brushes and toothpaste
- Hair dryer or other styling appliances
- Razor and shaving cream
- Hairbrush
- Deodorant
- Shampoo
- Soap
- Hair bands

Supplies

- Paper towels
- Wipes
- Tissues
- Travel pillows
- Overnight bag
- Laundry bag
- Sweaters for cold cars
- Towels
- Safety pins
- Matches or lighter (make sure they work)
- Mirror
- Superglue
- Poncho
- String
- Tape
- Spoon and fork

Medical Supplies

For Pain

- Motrin
- Tylenol
- Aspirin (not for use by teens or children)

For Colds

- Cough drops
- Decongestant (Benadryl liquid and tablets)

For Cuts and Sores

- Alcohol swabs
- Band-Aids
- Lip balm
- Calamine lotion
- Hydrocortisone cream
- Neosporin
- Molefoams with pain relief
- Sterile pads
- Sterile cotton
- Waterproof medical tape

For Digestion

- Antacid (Rolaids)
- Motion sickness pills
- Pepcid Complete

For Teeth and Mouth

- Chlorasaeptic mouth pain spray
- Orajel
- Tic Tacs or sugar-free mints

For Eyes

- Eye cup for flushing objects out of eye
- Eye dropper
- Eye ointment
- Visine, eye drops, Poly-trim opthalmic solution

For Bugs

- Calamine or cortisone for bug bites
- Mosquito repellent

For Allergies

- Benadryl
- Zyrtec

For Ears

- Earache medicine

For Sun

- Sunscreen
- Solarcaine Aloe Gel

Miscellaneous

- ACE bandage
- Tongue depressors
- Dosage dropper
- Tweezers
- First aid card or manual
- CPAP
- Synthroid
- Handkerchief
- CoQ10
- Iodine or water cleaner
- Vitamins
- Moist towelettes
- Backup meds
- Popsicle sticks
- PLAX
- Q-tips
- Walking stick
- Stay Awake
- Weighted ball
- Thermometer
- Massager

CHAPTER FIVE

Packing the Toys

My friend gave her kids a big ball of yarn and some children's scissors and invited them to make a spiderweb in the backseat. They strung yarn all over the car. It kept them busy for hours, and all she had to do to clean up was to snip all the knots and throw the yarn away. She said it was the best, cheapest car toy ever! —Kathryn

Most parents fear that kids and cars don't mix. That's why, whenever I mention that I've been on a long road trip, my listener exclaims with surprise, "But how did your kids do?"

When you're planning your itinerary, the hours you'll spend driving might sound like a terrible burden, with screaming children attacking each other from their secured car seats. But if you accept that the driving is a necessary part of the trip, and plan ahead to prepare ways to entertain and distract your children, you can turn the drive into a valuable addition to your family road trip.

COMFORT ITEMS

Keep your kids comfortable by bringing travel pillows, blankets, stuffed animals, or favorite toys. You'll keep them happier, and everybody will have a better drive. Make sure that each child has a pillow or something to lean on to make napping easier. When tired toddlers get much needed sleep, parents get much needed quiet! You'll also enjoy night driving better if your children can quietly doze while you drive, instead of screaming because they're getting so tired.

When you're deciding whether to bring favorite dolls or toys, remember that it's easy to lose things when you travel. Toys fall out of car doors, get left in hotels, or get dropped in busy crowds. Carefully consider the repercussions when you bring irreplaceable objects. Sometimes it might be better to leave a favorite toy or doll behind and bring the second best. If your child objects, explain that the special doll is going on its own trip, and make up stories about the doll's adventures.

NEW TOYS

Kids love toys, and novelty makes everything more exciting. Before your trip, consider buying some new trinkets for traveling. Look for things that are new to your kids so that they have a few happy hours before the novelty wears off. Look for small or travel-sized toys and gadgets like squeeze toys, brain puzzlers, tiny dolls, or cars that toddlers can drive around CarSeat Land. Bring a variety—you never know what your kids will love.

Travel toys don't have to be expensive. Most toy stores have bins of cheap trinkets, just the kind of small novelty a kid can enjoy for a few minutes before moving on to something else. You can also search thrift stores for travel toys. If you haven't spent a lot of money on your toys, you won't mind if they get stepped on and smashed, or lost at rest stops, as often happens with travel toys.

You can even design your own travel toys—the simpler the better!

I made a cheap magnet toy using a dollar store cookie sheet and some kiddie magnet sets. I use an old peanut butter jar to hold the magnets when not in use, and it's big enough that my daughter can reach her hand in to get magnets out. She can also tuck it to one side in her seat. —Kendra

Some parents like to wrap travel toys before they drive. This gives children something to look forward to and makes the toys more exciting. The unwrapping fills a few precious seconds, and every second you have happy children is one more second without screaming. Every second counts.

If you're traveling during Christmas, give travel toys for Christmas gifts. Your children will be set for their drives with new gadgets.

One Christmas my husband bought the kids a Perplexus, a three-dimensional maze inside a ball. They brought it in the car and spent hours trying to solve it. —Loralee

GAMES

If your children like games, look for a travel game set with magnetic pieces that won't slide off the board, like chess or checkers. For regular card games, make sure kids have a level place to put the cards, such as a flat box or a pie tin. Sometimes kids will spend more time playing a game like tic-tac-toe if they have a fancy game board for it. There are also games for single players, if your children like to play alone.

On the other hand, you can do a lot of games with pencil and paper (or with a litter-free magnetic drawing board). So don't forget the notepads!

COLORING

Kids love to draw, and the car is a perfect place to let them go to town. But pens and markers can stain car seats and clothes, while crayons can get mashed into seats or melt in hot cars. Should you bring them or not?

Coloring is a toughie, since a dropped crayon is more hassle than it's worth. So I glued strong magnets to some pen caps and use a cheap cookie sheet as a drawing surface. The pens stay on and you can use magnets to hold the paper in place. I stick magnets to the pen cap, since when a pen is being used it's the pen cap that usually gets lost, since the kids are holding the pen. Plus, as a pen wears out, I can just buy the same brand again and put the new pens into the old caps! —Kendra

One February, my husband found a new art product: Crayola window crayons. Our car windows soon sported flowers, airplane battles, mountain scenes, and autographs, and the crayons kept our kids entertained for hours of driving. But when they rediscovered the crayons in June, it didn't take long for warm crayon to get smudged onto clothing and melt into seat covers. From now on, these crayons will be for winters only! —Loralee

Crayola Color Wonder markers make a good travel alternative, whether you choose preprinted coloring books or blank paper tablets. Colored pencils are another good option, since they don't melt or bleed ink. (Don't forget the pencil sharpener!)

STICKERS

Stickers are surprisingly versatile, and they don't stain (unless you forget to check your laundry for stickers on clothes). Kids can use them to fill in drawings, create original art, or use them as tape. Look at Target or Fred Meyer for cheap sticker books or packages with hundreds of stickers.

> *My girls both love stickers. So sometimes we just give stickers (with and without paper), and sometimes we give them fancy restickable stickers that can go on a background. I also found printable Do-a-Dot letters online (letters made entirely of dots) that I slip in plastic sheet protectors. With a package of dot stickers from an office supply store, my girls can fill in the dots with stickers, unstick them, and restick them to their hearts' content. —Britney*

Sticker puzzles are nice activities for the car, because they're flat and they don't shed pieces. There is also a variety of sticker books, including books of state flags, strange animals, and foreign languages.

> *We bring Usborne Sticker Dolly Dressing books on car trips. My girls enjoy dressing the fairies or dancers in different sticker outfits. Some of books are even educational, like the one with costumes from around the world. —Amanda G.*

ACTIVITY BOOKS AND KITS

Activity books can fill up hours of time. Try crossword puzzles, mazes, sudoku, or educational workbooks like math books.

Instruction books also keep kids busy. Your kids might like books on how to fold origami or draw animals. They'll have plenty of time in the car to practice!

PROJECTS

Does your child have an uncompleted project or an unopened activity kit? Bring it along. Hours spent traveling can be a good time to learn a new skill, like making friendship bracelets, or to finish a project, like a year-old cross-stitch. Even tiny kids enjoy "sewing" with needles and thread, and if they're not trying to make something specific, it doesn't matter when the sewing goes awry.

> *My older two children were trying to sew car pillows, so my three-year-old wanted to join in. She determinedly pushed her needle through the cloth, handing it over every so often for untangling, and then went back to work. Finally, she tugged at the needle and pulled the thread so tight that the whole fabric bunched up into a solid mass. "Look, Mommy,"* *she exclaimed, "I made a ball!" —Loralee*

LEARNING OPPORTUNITIES

When they're stuck in the car for hours, your children are a captive audience. Some parents like to put this time to practical use with maps, flash cards, workbooks, or silly car games that teach as you go. There's also an app to teach anything: math games, spelling games, and even music note recognition. This time is especially useful if your children have homework like memorizing multiplication tables.

You can also seize learning opportunities as they come. Add up numbers on license plates for a fun math exercise or look at maps of your route. Travel is all about learning.

If you try to educate your children as you go, be sure to keep it fun. Play silly learning games or reward your kids with stickers or time with electronics. Be sensitive to your children's moods, and don't force them to participate if they're worn out. You'll just ruin the drive.

Our children wanted to play on the touchpads all day, so we made an agreement. To earn ten minutes on the touchpad, they each had to memorize a short verse. They'd learned eight by the end of the day. —Loralee

COINS

Bring a bag of change to use with kids in the car. You might hand out coins for good behavior or as rewards for car games. You can also fine misbehavior by confiscating coins when kids scream or hit. It's also handy to have change in the car in case you need to use a parking meter, pass a tollbooth, or find a pay phone when your cell phone dies.

LIGHTS

Will your kids need lights for nighttime traveling? Consider buying them flashlights or headlamps. If your child wiggles so much that the headlamp will shine around the car and distract the driver, try looping it around the seat in front to make a dangling lamp. You can also try a lamp that attaches to the car, or car seats with activity lights in the headrest.

BOOKS

Books make a great travel treat. Stock up on used books at Half Price Books, Goodwill, or other thrift stores where most children's books cost less than a dollar. Take your kids shopping with you and let them choose their own books. Thrift stores are also a great place to find cheap activity books or coloring books. (You can always rip out any precolored pages.)

At the thrift store, look for paperback copies of your children's favorite picture books. Paperbacks are smaller and flatter than hardcover copies, so you can pack more of them in, and you'll be able to read your children their familiar stories without the danger of losing expensive hardbound editions.

Before we travel, we take our kids shopping for books at Goodwill. We let the kids choose; sometimes they find a geology book or a book about a state we're going to or a blank journal. Don't just herd them to the children's book section. My son especially loves Guinness Books of World Records. He can always find them at Goodwill, and he doesn't care what year they're from. —Rachel

The I SPY books from Scholastic are great, since even if your kids can't read, they can see what items they're searching for. Any "seek and find" books like that are great, but the I SPY ones are small and easy to hold and keep in a basket in the car. —Kendra

MUSIC

Does your family have favorite pop songs, folk songs, silly songs, or church songs? If your kids like to sing, bring music for family sing-alongs.

My husband and I buy used CDs for cheap, CDs we loved as kids so we know they're clean. Then, when we're in the car, we can introduce the kids to something we know they'll like. Our kids are now singing "Karma Chameleon" and "Istanbul." —Rachel

Even if you don't have recordings, you can still sing. Brush up on your favorite lyrics before you go, or bring a book of song lyrics to give you an easy way to entertain kids in the car.

One Christmas Eve, on our annual drive to visit family in Utah, we drove straight into a snowstorm. As we crawled along at stop-and-go pace, I led the kids through every winter snow song I could think of. It kept us going for two hours.
—Loralee

AUDIOBOOKS

When you're traveling together, it's fun to share the same experiences. That's one reason that many families enjoy listening together to music, storytelling, audiobooks, or CDs of old TV shows.

Look for audiobooks at your local library, or join Audible.com to buy recordings of popular books. You can also download free audiobooks from Librivox.org.

When you're packing books, bring extras. No matter how wonderful you think they might be, many audiobooks fail to engage. The reader's voice might put you to sleep or rub you the wrong way. A book that sounded exciting might bore you stiff. There might be profanity, violence, or crude behavior you don't want your children to listen to. Whatever the reason, bring enough so that you can set the boring book aside and try a better one.

Audiobooks for the Whole Family
- *Skulduggery Pleasant* by Derek Landy
- Rick Riordan books
- Agatha Christie mystery novels
- *Harry Potter* books by J.K. Rowling
- *The Alloy of Law* by Brandon Sanderson
- *Charlotte's Web* by E.B. White
- *Snow Treasure* by Marie McSwigan

- *Little House on the Prairie* books by Laura Ingalls Wilder
- *Al Capone Does My Shirts* by Gennifer Choldenko
- *The Penderwicks* by Jeanne Birdsall
- *The Willoughbys* by Lois Lowry
- *Icefall* by Matthew J. Kirby
- *The Sea of Trolls* by Nancy Farmer
- *Garlic and Sapphires* by Ruth Reichl
- Carl Hiassen's books *Hoot, Flush*, and *Scat*
- *Arabel's Raven* and other books by Joan Aiken such as *Armitage, Armitage, Fly Away Home* or *The Serial Garden.*
- *Hank the Cowdog* by John R. Erickson

Storytellers the Whole Family Can Enjoy

- Bill Harley
- Bil Lepp
- Carmen Deedy
- Willy Claflin
- Tim Tingle
- Donald Davis

Librivox Audiobooks

- The *Oz* books by Frank L. Baum
- *A Christmas Carol* by Charles Dickens
- *Alice in Wonderland* by Lewis Carroll
- E. Nesbit books
- *The Peterkin Papers* by Lucretia P. Hale
- *Anne of Green Gables* and sequels by L. M. Montgomery
- Folk tales from many cultures

This website is always adding new books to its collection, so browse the site. You'll find lots of treasures, and they're all free.

ELECTRONICS

If you're worried that your books, toys, and games will be scattered all over the car by the end of your trip, consider switching to electronics. With today's technology, you can take a laptop, an iPad, or an iPhone and fill it with e-books, games, and all sorts of possibilities to keep kids quiet. Plan ahead so that you can download the right games, books, and music before you go.

POLICIES

You're the parent, and you paid for the gadgets, so you get to make the rules. If you don't want the children using electronics every minute of your drive, decide ahead of time what your policy on electronics will be. Will each child have a device, or will they share? Will they be trading? Will you set a time limit? Will you rely on toys and books for entertainment and pull out the devices only for emergency boredom relief? Plan ahead so that you can explain the rules to your children, and warn them that gadgets will need to be turned off if they're distracting the driver.

You should also check your data plan and tell your children what features they can and cannot use. Are they allowed to download data or stream movies? You may need to block downloading or other actions.

VIDEOS

Some parents play movies as they drive to keep their children quiet. If your car has a DVD player installed, you're set. If not, you can buy an inexpensive DVD player. Make sure you bring movies you don't mind hearing (a movie that quiets the children won't be any good if it annoys the parents), or bring headphones for the children.

Before you plan on using DVDs for the entire trip, consider what else you can do. Bring some quiet activities and see how your children enjoy them. You might be surprised at how much fun you can have without a DVD playing, and you'll always have it in reserve.

When we drove from Seattle to Arizona, we loaded several movies onto our iPod because we were worried about how our kids would handle such a long trip. We shouldn't have. They forgot that the movies were available and just enjoyed their books and activities. I don't think we watched a single movie. —Loralee

If your car has a DVD player, you could also bring a game system. Keep it as a backup, or let your children play whenever they need entertainment.

When we drove from Utah to Washington, we brought the Wii to use with our in-car DVD player. (The Wii required less power than our Xbox, and we had to bring a power inverter to run it.) While my wife drove, I played Guitar Hero *and* Lego Indiana Jones *with my five-year-old son and his two older cousins. It kept them happy the entire way! —Josh*

PACKING IT ALL IN

Pockets attached to seatbacks make great organizers for young passengers. There they can store toys, books, writing and drawing supplies, snacks, water bottles, and anything else they might want during the trip. This, in turn, can keep seat and floor areas clear.

Some cars come with seat pockets. If your car doesn't, you can buy some ready-made. Alternatively, you can adapt a multipocket apron or jacket to create pocket designs for each car and for each child's needs.

When I was a girl, my family moved from Utah to Texas. With six kids and a dog in the car, my mom had to be creative! She prepared a blanket for the trip with pockets full of toys and treats, kind of like an advent calendar. She stretched it across the back of her seat so that kids could reach it. Twice a day, each of us got to choose something from a pocket. It gave us something to look forward to, and then something to enjoy as we drove. —Amanda G.

If you don't have seat pockets, pack each child's toys, books, and other entertainment in a small bag or backpack that can be stowed on the seat or under their feet.

When we travel, I have my boys pack their own activity backpacks. Whatever they want to bring, they pack themselves. Then, when we drive, each of them has a backpack within easy reach. —Colette

TRAVEL-TESTED CAR ACTIVITIES

It was all new stuff, and none of it was expensive. —Raissa

- Invisible ink pens
- Perplexus
- Sticker books about states
- Stickers
- Slinky
- Super Tooobs (Plastic accordion tube toys that kids can turn into games, jump ropes, or intercom systems)
- Recorders
- Tin whistles
- Printouts of lyrics for learning popular songs
- Sticker puzzles
- Sticker book of Spanish words
- Origami
- Friendship bracelet kit
- Cross-stitch project
- Supplies for sewing pillows
- Dollar store coloring kit with coloring book, stickers, and crayons
- Usborne Sticker Dolly books
- New pack of Uno cards
- Monopoly Millionaire (played in pie tins to contain the stacks of cards)
- Dry-erase crayons for coloring windows
- Notebook with four-color pen on a string for drawing or playing games
- Blokus travel game

CHAPTER SIX

Food and Snacks

When we travel, we like to use our almost-expired seventy-two-hour kits. We take trips in the summer and for the winter holidays, which is roughly every six months, so we pack stuff in the kits that will last for six months. So far, my kids hate tuna salad packets, fruit snacks, peanuts, and raisins. They like the cheese and cracker snacks, 100 percent juice boxes, and Fruit Roll-Ups. They also liked the canned spam and turkey spam sliced into cubes, but you have to pack a plate and knife. —Susan

When you're preparing for your trip, think about what you'll be eating. What will you feed your children for snacks? For meals? Do you need to pack food for rest stops or for meals when you stop? If you think ahead, you can avoid food problems and be prepared.

SNACKS

Snack time is a great time in the car. Kids quiet down as they munch, and you can stave off hunger complaints, especially if you're well-prepared.

It's nice to have a variety of foods in the car. Not only will this keep the kids more interested but they'll get more full if you feed them different kinds of food. You can bring things like crackers, nuts, pretzels, sliced cheese, sliced fruit, drinks, premade peanut butter sandwiches, or whatever else you can think of. Be creative—maybe your favorite boxed cereal will make a good car snack.

Choosing Healthy Options

Think carefully about what foods you're serving—some are better than others! Most snack foods, including crackers, Goldfish snacks, pretzels, or beef jerky, contain extra salt. Not only can this be bad for everybody's health but it can cause your children to beg for lots of drinks and lead to extra bathroom stops. Many snack foods like granola bars or gummy fruit snacks have lots of added sugar. So do treats like cookies.

When you're choosing crackers or bread, look for whole grain options. Not only are these more nutritious but they're also more filling. Cut down on salt by buying low-sodium crackers and unsalted nuts. For fruit snacks, look for actual dried fruit, like dried raisins and apples, instead of sugar-laden fruit rolls or gummy fruit snacks. Even better, bring fresh fruit or veggies, which are more filling than dried options. Grapes, baby tomatoes, slices of apples, celery, or peppers add a nice burst of flavor to a cracker snack. They'll also help fill children up.

We bring a veggie tray when we drive, along with the typical granola bars, pretzels, almonds, cheese sticks, rice cakes, etc. We also like some fresh fruit along the way. —Emily

Snacks for the Driver

Snacks can help keep the driver alert. Whether you choose caffeinated drinks, favorite cookies for munching, strong mints like chewing gum or Altoids, or spicy treats like wasabi almonds, consider what the driver needs when you're packing your snacks. (You don't have to share these with the kids, but you might want to bring kid-appropriate substitutes to pass out when they want the grown-up treats.)

Containers

When you're passing out snacks, minimize the mess by serving food in containers like small plates, cups, or bowls. These will catch crumbs and spills.

We save small yogurt containers and pack them with our trip food. I use them for snack containers or water cups, wash them when we stop, and throw them away if they break. —Loralee

You can also pack the food ahead of time in resealable or divided containers. This will make it even easier to hand out at snack time.

Packing snacks in a divided lunch container like the Goodbyn Byntos or EasyLunchboxes is great because they're easy to pass around in the car from whoever is in charge of the cooler bag, and they rest nicely on a lap while riding. And they prevent the impulsive fast-food stop! Wash them and use them to store leftovers from restaurants on your trip, or bring your own lunches and snacks to an amusement park or someplace like that, depending on your destination. —Kendra

Drinks

Drinks like soda and fruit juice can contain more sugar than candy bars. These can also cause stains when they spill. Juice boxes are handy, but small children are likely to squeeze the containers and accidentally squirt juice everywhere. To cut down on sugar and spills, parents can look for small or diet drinks, or serve the simplest drink of all: water.

One easy way to supply drinks for your kids is to pack a water bottle for each child. Make sure these are bottles the children can open themselves and that won't tip and spill too easily. However, some children might drink too much if they have their own water bottles. In this case, you can pour water into cups and serve smaller amounts.

> When we drove to Colorado this summer, my four-year-old drank up most of her water bottle before we noticed what she was doing. We were pulling over for bathroom stops all afternoon—sometimes in very inconvenient places! —Loralee

GUM

Some parents love gum for car trips, and some parents hate it. On the one hand, gum can help clean teeth (especially if it's sugar free or contains Xylitol). It pops ears at high altitudes. Kids can enjoy gum for a long time, and it keeps them from begging for snacks. On the other hand, if kids drop their gum, it makes a sticky mess!

> We always take gum on car trips. It gives the kids something to do, and it helps the kids pop their ears when we're driving over mountain passes. —Rachel

My mom went through a period when she passed out gum on every car trip. She raved about it to her friends, telling them how the gum didn't make kids thirsty, so it cut down on drinks and bathroom stops. Then a piece of gum got stuck to a seat belt and was a huge pain to clean up. She never gave us gum in the car again. —Loralee

Think About Your Teeth

When you're traveling, you're probably not concentrating on dental care. Unless you're stopping frequently to brush teeth, think carefully about the snacks you choose for your kids.

- Sticky candy, such as jelly beans, can get stuck to crevices in teeth and contribute to cavities.
- Dried fruit, such as raisins, can also contribute to cavities if it gets stuck in teeth, because it's sticky and also contains sugar.
- Food containing carbohydrates, such as crackers, can get stuck in teeth, get broken down into sugars, and contribute to cavities.
- Fresh fruit does not contribute to cavities. Some kinds of fruit, such as apples, can help clean teeth.
- Chewing sugar-free gum can help prevent cavities.

Spills

Avoid packing food that will stain clothes and upholstery or make a crumbly mess. Spilled juice will leave a sticky stain, and spilled milk can sour and stink. Chocolate can melt and seep into fabric. Greasy food like potato chips can leave oil spots on fabric. Graham crackers and Triscuits scatter crumbs when they shatter. Crackers or chips with a cheesy coating might stain fingers orange.

No matter what precautions you take, spills will always happen. Pack plenty of paper towels and baby wipes.

MEALS

Whether you eat in the car or stop for fast food, people are going to need real meals. You might want to pack enough to feed everybody in the car without stopping. You might stop for fast food or someplace quick to give children a chance to stretch their legs, use the restroom, and get out the wiggles. Whichever you choose, be prepared to supply breakfast, lunch, and dinner.

Packing Food

It's great to start a trip with a cooler full of sandwiches. You can eat what you like when you like and not have to stop for fast food. If you keep dry ice in your cooler or bring an electric cooler that plugs into the car, you can carry perishable items for several days. (If you can't keep it cold, don't pack perishable food.)

Another alternative is to take snacks that won't spoil rapidly, like sliced fruit or presliced cheese. You can also take sandwich toppings like peanut butter or canned tuna and make fresh sandwiches when you stop.

I try to always have a variety of snacks in case I need to feed my kids "dinner" if we're driving through the middle of nowhere. With sliced cheese, apples, and crackers, I can approximate a meal, at least for my kids, or round it off with some raisins and nuts. —Loralee

Fast Food

Fast-food sandwiches from the dollar menu can be a good way to quickly feed your kids. But fast food often contains too much fat, salt, or sugar. Even "healthy" items can be deceiving;

for instance, a McDonald's serving of five chicken nuggets has more fat and almost as much salt as a small hamburger. If you buy fast food, consider supplementing with a healthy side like fresh fruit.

When you buy fast food, get what you want. Don't be afraid to order sandwiches without messy condiments or with extra pickles for pickle lovers. If you're splitting sandwiches among children, ask for the sandwiches to be cut in pieces, or ask for a knife so that you can divide them yourself. You can also ask for extra napkins in case of spills.

One word of advice: watch out for dips and condiments. If your children must eat their French fries with ketchup or dip their chicken pieces in barbecue sauce, consider eating in the restaurant instead of in the car. You don't want ketchup all over car seats!

STOPS

If you plan on picnicking, you can pack things you might not want to eat in the car. It's also easier to eat messy food, or eat with utensils, when you're out of the car. A picnic stop is a great time to serve yogurt or cereal, make sandwiches, cut apples, or serve up anything else you don't want in the car.

If you're planning a picnic, don't forget

- Utensils
- Something to eat out of: paper plates, washable dishes, or fast-food containers
- Napkins and wipes for cleanup

One of our craziest food stops was coming home from a beach trip. We still had a carton of ice cream that we hadn't used, so we put it in our cooler. But when we stopped at a nearby beach park, we saw that it was already melting. We didn't have any spoons, but we did have a container of sliced apples. We passed out apples and told our kids to use them to eat the ice cream. That's the only time I've ever heard my husband say, "Eat the ice cream, not the apples!" —Loralee

MEALS FOR LONG TRIPS

If you're planning a long camping trip or a trip in which you need to provide all the meals, figure out what you're planning to take.

- Ingredients for cooking (don't forget seasonings like salt, pepper, or oil, and don't forget the recipes)
- Utensils
- Sandwich ingredients (don't forget condiments)
- Food made ahead and packed in a cooler, such as lasagna, ribs, meat loaf (or buy premade versions to Heat up when you're there)
- Canned food with can openers

We packed all our own food when we traveled to Glacier National Park: milk, cereal, and bananas for breakfast, sandwich stuff for lunch, hot dogs for dinner, and lots of yummy chips and snacks. We ended up spending only what we would have spent on food at home. The problem was that we were entering bear country, with scary signs warning us not to leave smelly food scraps that would attract bears, so we had to eat our potato chips in the car! —Loralee

If you're planning to take all of your own food instead of buying food onsite, check ahead of time to make sure your vacation site has everything you need. If you'll be staying at a cabin, will you have a refrigerator, freezer, barbecue, oven, stove, pots and pans, plates, and utensils? What about dishwashing liquid, paper towels, and other cleaning supplies? If you plan on cooking your own food in a motel room, will you have a microwave?

If you're camping, will you be able to light a campfire and find firewood? (Many sites now ask that you use local wood instead of bringing your own to avoid importing pests.)

For dietary and financial reasons, we did a lot of our own cooking while on the road. But not every motel we stayed at had a way to cook, and storing food was also an issue. So we would usually take along a small microwave and a car cooler that would plug into our cigarette lighter. It gave us a lot more eating flexibility. —Rick

NO MATTER WHAT

Whether you're packing every meal, stopping to buy every meal, or doing something in between, bring extra food. You might need to feed your family an emergency meal if your budget motel doesn't offer breakfast, or you miss dinner driving through a wilderness with no fast food in sight, or your cooler fails and your perishable food warms up to dangerous levels. Fruit, cereal, granola bars, bread and cheese, and milk boxes are all good fallback options.

CHAPTER SEVEN

Last-Minute Tasks before Leaving the House

Sometimes it takes so long to get through last-minute tasks, I feel as if I'm trudging through quicksand. There's always one more toy to grab, one more apple to cut, one more curtain to close, or one child to send to the bathroom. Even getting in the car doesn't always mean we're ready to go—many times we've started driving only to circle the block and return for sunglasses or water bottles or books on CD. But eventually we're able to hit the road, and it always feels great! —Loralee

PLANNING YOUR DEPARTURE

As the time to leave approaches, decide how you're going to travel. Families do this many different ways:

- Leave at 4:00 a.m. to let kids sleep in the car.
- Leave early enough to drive all day and still have time for activities.
- Leave after work and drive late into the night.

- Drive all night while children sleep.

Whatever your plan, allow extra time for rest stops, meals, or emergencies. Everything takes longer when you're traveling with children. And, unless you're a genuine night owl, don't drive too late at night for safety's sake.

PACKING THE CAR

If you're leaving early in the morning, pack your luggage in the car the night before. Leave electronics and valuables to pack in the morning, but make sure you have space for them. You will be amazed at how long it takes to get everything in!

Once you've packed everything in your car or in your top carrier, check to make sure the driver has good visibility. Don't block the back window!

GETTING READY

Make sure your food is ready to go. Do you need to make sandwiches and put them in the fridge for the next day? Do you need to refrigerate drinks so you'll have cold drinks for the road? Do you need to slice fruit or buy vegetables? Do you have ice or cold packs for your cooler?

If you plan to leave early in the morning, decide whether to feed kids before you leave or pack breakfast for the car. You may also want to lay out everybody's clothes to make the morning go faster.

LAST-MINUTE TASKS

As you're preparing to leave the house, go back one more time to sweep the house and make sure everything is taken care of.

- Look for anything you forgot to pack.
- Check your fridge to make sure you haven't left your travel food.
- Take care of perishable food. Freeze or throw away leftovers. Give away food that might go bad, such as milk, bread, or produce.
- Lock doors and windows.
- Make sure that sliding doors and windows have a bar or extra lock to keep them from being jimmied and slid open.
- If you have a home security system, turn on the alarm before you leave.
- Turn off lights and turn down the heat or air conditioning.
- Send your children to the bathroom one last time— they'll be asking to go again far too soon!

CHAPTER EIGHT

Managing the Drive

*Once, our kids, sitting in the back of the minivan, started
yelling at each other in a game that got louder and crazier.
My husband and I couldn't reach them or make them stop,
and the noise was driving us nuts. In desperation, I turned
on Adele's "Rolling in the Deep," and within seconds we were
all singing at the top of our lungs. By redirecting the noise,
we managed to turn a trip-ruining moment into a happy
memory. —Loralee*

Forget napping. Forget turning on your grownup-level audiobook, or hearing the words if you do. Forget the Zen quiet of
road hum, of meditating on the peaceful scenery as you pass.
After all, you're traveling with kids.

Traveling with children is a full-time job. You'll probably
have snacks to pass out, fights to break up, games to suggest, and
picture books to read (or recite, if your children are holding the
books somewhere behind you). On the other hand, you'll have

time to play games, listen to audiobooks, sing together, and talk about things of great importance or no importance at all.

Your family vacation starts when you get in the car, not when you arrive at your destination. If you can drive safely while helping your children when they need entertainment, food, and parental involvement, you can enjoy your family time together instead of letting it degenerate into free-for-all screaming that aggravates everyone.

PRIORITIZING NEEDS

When you're traveling, everybody needs to be kept happy. But who is first priority? Who gets to choose the music or when to stop? Who is number one?

If you have a baby, the baby is number one. You can't negotiate when babies need to eat, sleep, or be changed. You can't reason or bribe babies out of screaming. You travel around their schedules and drive as far as you can when they're napping.

Otherwise, the driver's needs have first priority, since the lives of the entire family are in the driver's hands. If a certain tune or radio show keeps the driver alert, that's what you listen to. If the driver needs to stop and stretch, rest, or get a refill, then you stop. If the driver needs something while driving, such as snacks, new music, sunglasses, or directions, someone else needs to take care of it.

If there are two adults in the car, the nondriver needs to keep the children happy and quiet so that the driver doesn't get frustrated or distracted. Try to prevent complaints and fights instead of letting them escalate until everybody's upset. You might do this by singing songs, playing games, telling stories, or starting conversations and listening to your children's responses. You might even need to sit next to a fussy child or toddler and try finger-plays, funny faces, picture books, squeaky toys, or whatever else you have in your arsenal. (See entertainment ideas below.)

If you're planning to switch drivers, the backup driver may need to recharge, take a nap, or have some sort of break from kid duties. Buy some quiet time by passing out snacks or new toys, or putting on a new audiobook or your children's favorite music. You might also try the quiet game and ask your children to find quiet activities to do. If you have young children who sleep in the car, you can grab a nap for yourself.

TRAVELING ALONE

If you're a single parent or the only adult on the trip, figure out ways for your children to help themselves while you travel.

- Put snacks where kids can reach them, and don't be surprised if they eat everything within reach.
- Choose music or an audiobook that you and your children can both enjoy.
- Assign an older child to pass out toys or snacks or to entertain siblings.
- Make sure you can reach the things you need, such as snacks, drinks, or tissues.

Even when you're driving alone, you can help distract or entertain your children. Invite them to tell you a story, play the ABC game, call out exotic license plates, guess letters for hangman, or ask them to watch the road signs and tell you how far it is to the next town. Even better, start some sort of game they can play themselves.

One winter I drove to Seattle from Utah with my two-year-old, since my wife had already flown home with the baby. The weather was terrible, and storms had closed the mountain passes, so we had to take a long detour. I gave my daughter a bottle of water and a bag of Goldfish crackers, and we just drove. —Laramie

SNACKS AND DRINKS

Who's going to be in charge of the snacks? Will you give each child a snack bag, or pass out servings at regular intervals? Will you give each child a water bottle?

If you're not ready to pass out snacks when your children start asking for them, invite them to wait for a few minutes and tell them what numbers to watch for on the clock. Tell them that at that time you'll pass out snacks, but only if they don't keep begging until then. If they continue to beg, move the time forward.

HOUSEKEEPING

As your children unwrap snacks and juice boxes and generate pages of artwork, trash starts to pile up. Keep a designated garbage container somewhere in the car, such as an empty snack box, or a plastic grocery bag tied to a door handle. Ask all passengers (including grownups) to put garbage in the container as soon as possible, instead of throwing it on the floor. If you make it easy to dispose of trash, your car will stay relatively clutter free.

TOYS, GAMES, AND PROJECTS

If you've got new things for the children to enjoy, try spacing them out over time. This will give your children time to appreciate and enjoy each new plaything.

When we go on car trips, we prepare a bag of treats and toys from the dollar store. Then, every hour, we hand out something new. It keeps the kids interested—and busy!
—Adam

Even after your best planning, sometimes the toys, games, and projects lose their appeal. If your children aren't enjoying their playthings, here are some things you can try:

- For toddlers who are refusing their toys, play with the toys yourself. Talk on toy phones, send cars driving down your arm and over the dashboard, or squeeze squeaky toys. Even better, rave to the driver about how much fun you're having. Your toddler will soon be begging for what suddenly looks like a really fun toy.
- Play with your kids. Participate in a game of cards or tic-tac-toe, or ask if you can help make pictures with stickers.
- Help out. If your children are fighting over the rules of a game, help them figure it out. If somebody's having trouble with a project, see what you can do to help. Both you and your kids will be much happier if they can work successfully on something they can be proud of, instead of giving up in tears because it's too hard.

My kids have done lots of great projects in the car, which puts me in charge of crisis management. I've had to unpick misplaced embroidery stitches, untangle sewing knots, start friendship bracelets, consult on origami instructions, start pipe cleaner braids, unbraid waxy Wikki Stix, and help indecisive artists choose colors. This helps my kids do something they can't do otherwise, and everybody's happier.
—Loralee

SIMPLE IDEAS FOR FAMILY FUN

There are lots of ways to enjoy drive time without using toys. The more ideas you have in your arsenal, the more prepared you'll be to distract and entertain your children.

Songs

Many children love to sing. You can keep it interesting by changing things up or turning old songs into new games. For instance, how many animals can you think of for Old MacDonald? What sound would you make for a parrot, a porcupine, or a porpoise? The longer the song goes, the sillier it gets.

You could also try making up new lyrics to familiar tunes. "Twinkle, Twinkle, Little Star" might become something like, "We are driving in a car." For an even bigger challenge, one person can make up two lines of a song, and the next person comes up with a rhyming passage.

Games with physical activity keep children especially occupied. Try a song like, "If You're Happy and You Know It, Clap Your Hands." Make up new actions, like "stomp your feet," "wiggle your nose," "tap your toes." Or you can make up new moods: "If you're hungry and you know it," "If you're sad and you know it," "If you're sleepy and you know it."

Other fun sing-along songs:
- The Hokey Pokey
- Popcorn Popping
- Head, Shoulders, Knees and Toes
- I'm Bringing Home a Baby Bumblebee
- This Is the Way (we wash our face, brush our hair, etc.)
- The Wheels on the Bus
- Do As I'm Doing

Sing-Along Music

One preschool teacher loves these singers for entertaining young children:

- Charlotte Diamond (she sings "Slippery Fish," among others)
- Greg and Steve
- Tickle Toon Typhoon
- Sandra Boynton
- Nancy Stewart

You can even find sing-along music about car trips, like John Denver's "Country Roads" or the Indigo Girls' "Power of Two."

For some variety, try classical music. Children love music with vivid imagery, like "Flight of the Bumblebee" or *The 1812 Overture*. Vivaldi's *Four Seasons* is also a good choice for children, especially if you talk about how the different movements relate to the four seasons, and what might be happening with each piece.

Musicals that tell a story are another good way to keep kids interested for a long period of time, especially if it's a story they know. A lot of classic musicals have music that's fun to sing along with, and a musical like *Les Misérables* might keep your children entranced for hours.

One car trip, we introduced the children to Les Misérables *(making sure, of course, to skip the coarsest songs!) Not only were they soon singing "Look Down, Look Down" and other songs but they started picking out the melodies on my smartphone piano app. It kept them entertained for hours!*
—Loralee

Books and Stories

Audiobooks

Whether you put on something just for the grownups or for the whole family, listening to an exciting story is a good way to pass the time. If you run out of audiobooks on the road, try downloading new ones from Librivox.org or Audible.com. (See audiobook suggestions in chapter five.)

Reading Aloud

You can also try reading to each other in the car. It's a wonderful way to share your voices and pass the time, and it's good reading practice for younger children. These books are especially fun for family reading:

- *Skippyjon Jones* by Judy Schachner
- *Captain Underpants* or *Dragon Gets By* by Dav Pilkey
- *Hank the Cowdog* by John R. Erickson
- *Charlie and the Chocolate Factory* and other books by Roald Dahl
- The Bromeliad Trilogy: *Truckers*, *Diggers*, and *Wings* by Terry Pratchett
- The Chronicles of Narnia series by C.S. Lewis
- *Keys to the Kingdom* series by Garth Nix
- *Alcatraz Versus the Evil Librarians* series by Brandon Sanderson
- Harry Potter series by J.K. Rowling

Storytelling

Another option for stories is to make up family stories. You might take turns going around the car, with everybody contributing a word, a sentence, or a scene. If your children are too young to help tell the story, ask them for ideas of what happens next and then weave them into the story yourself. You can also make up stories about fantastical adventures that happen to your children or to toys at home. Children won't be so homesick for favorite toys if they know their beloved friends are having adventures of their own.

> *Once, I had the idea of telling a "group" story about characters that my boys and I had been telling stories about for a few years. But if you try to go in rotation, young kids usually don't come up with anything very elaborate. So I found the best way to play the game is to encourage the child to think of something outrageous or nutty that the character does and then the adult tries to fit it into the story. —Michael*

Make up stories about the area you're passing. Tell tall tales about how the landscape was created, make up stories about the people who might be living in the houses, or think about what your life would be like if you lived there.

> *On one car ride with my six-year-old granddaughter, we started talking about all the different houses. I'd tell her stories about the places we passed, like "If you lived on this farm, you might have a pony. You'd come home from school, feed the pony, and go for a ride." —Cheryl*

Timed talking: give each child a minute to talk about something, like the color red. See what they come up with and how long they can keep it up!

Games

Pencil and Paper Games
Some of the best games are also the simplest. All you need are paper and pencils.

- Tic-tac-toe
- Hangman

- Battleship: Each player draws a 10 × 10 grid, numbered on one side and lettered on the top. The players each mark five ships on their own grids: two that are 2 squares long, one 3 long, one 4 long, and one 5 long. Align the ships horizontally, vertically, or diagonally. To take a turn, a player guesses three squares, and the opponent must say whether each guess is a hit or miss. Both players should mark the location of every guess (this helps players avoid repeating their guesses). The first person to find all of the opponent's ships wins.
- Scribble: one person starts with a very simple drawing, such as a curve, a squiggle, a zigzag. The other person adds on to this squiggle to turn it into a picture.
- Drawing: invite children to draw what you're passing (e.g., "We're in the mountains—draw a mountain!"). This can also help you divide the journey into sections to help your children see how far they've come.

On one long car trip, I decided to try hangman with my daughter, who was almost five. I made boards and let her guess letters. Eventually, she said, "Mommy, I want to try." "But you don't know any words," I pointed out. "I know a few words," she said. She laboriously drew nine blanks on her page. Within a few guesses, I knew what it was: her name, the only nine-letter word she knew. —Loralee

Observation Games

If you can get your children looking out the windows and enjoying the scenery, so much the better. Here are some classic "look, look" games to try with your kids.

- ABC: Try to find the letters of the alphabet in order. Look for letters on billboards, store names, highway signs, or anywhere else you see print. (Hint: For really hard letters, like X and Z, scan license plates.) You can also try this with numbers.

- I Spy: Somebody chooses something visible outside (such as a windmill, restaurant, or grain harvester). Everybody else asks yes or no questions to try to figure out which object it is.

- Scavenger Hunt: Choose an object and invite your kids to watch for it out the window. You can choose something on the road, a kind of car, something you know is coming up (like a landmark), or whatever you want. This game works especially well if you already know which landmarks you're going to pass. You can either announce scavenger hunt sights one at a time or list several that children need to watch for.

- Maps: Some children will enjoy tracking your progress on maps. Pick up free maps at tourist stops, rest stops, tourist offices, or chambers of commerce, and show your children the route you're taking. They'll learn some geography as they go.

- License Plate Game: Watch license plates to find cars from as many states as you can. Pay special attention to trucks—you'll be surprised by how far some of them have traveled. You'll have the best success visiting national landmarks, such as national parks, that attract visitors from all over the country.

When we drove to Mount Rushmore, we found about seven rare license plates just by driving around the parking garage. We couldn't find Connecticut there, but we ran into three when we made an impromptu stop at Devils Tower! —Loralee

Math Games

You can do all sorts of things with numbers as you drive. For a child who has to learn the multiplication tables, call out the first two numbers on license plates and ask the child to multiply them. You can also do this for addition practice.

If your children enjoy thinking about distance and speed, have them guess how far it is to a certain point ahead or how long it will take to get there. They can also check highway signs to find how far it is to the next landmark and then use your driving speed to calculate how long it will take to get there. International travel provides even more opportunities to mention math. Canadian children might be astonished at how much longer it takes to drive 100 miles than 100 kilometers, while American children might think they're zooming when you drive 100 kilometers per hour (a sedate 62 mph).

You can also use math in stories to keep your children's attention.

> When we took car trips, I used to make up stories with numbers. It would be something like, "Two cats each had a litter of twelve kittens. Then each kitten grew up and had two more kittens. Half of the kittens ran away to live on a far-off mountain. How many cats were left?" The kids had to keep track and do the math to figure out how many there were. The key was to make the stories really silly—the sillier the better, because that's how you get kids to pay attention. —Cheryl

ELECTRONICS

Some families like to use electronics, such as movies, laptops, smartphones, and tablets, to keep kids occupied. Other families try to limit electronic usage or save it for special privileges.

Whatever your policy, decide ahead of time so that you can warn your children.

> *On one car trip, I wondered how to help my children practice music-note recognition. A piano teacher we visited suggested some smartphone apps. The next day, I downloaded two of them, and we had our children practice notes before they got to play other computer games, like Sudoku or Plants versus Zombies. Since one of the practice games was a note asteroid blaster, they didn't mind too much! —Loralee*

If the children will be sharing, help them negotiate how and when they'll trade. That might prevent later arguments. You might also have to help them keep track of time or gently reinforce when it's time to swap.

Sometimes you can use electronics to keep children alert at the right time.

> *Portable DVD player, iPad, Mobigo, iPhone . . . I use interactive electronics if I need my little girl to stay awake on the drive. —Kendra*

On the other hand, a quiet movie might help children settle down at naptime, as long as it doesn't put the parents to sleep!

Electronics are especially useful for nighttime, when it's too dark to look out the window or read books. Since the screens are lit, children can play games without turning on lights that will distract the driver.

Children also love using cameras, and taking pictures out of the window helps to pass the time. They'll enjoy choosing their own shots, focusing, and pushing buttons. You might even end up with some really fun travel pictures from your children's point of view. Liven up the drive with a photography contest:

everybody gets five chances to take the best picture of cows, mountains, a barn, or a highway sign.

MOTION SICKNESS

Motion sickness can occur when the motion your body feels doesn't match the motion your eyes see. If someone in your family is prone to car queasiness, these ideas might help keep your family from having to make an unscheduled stop to clean out your car and clean off your passengers.

- Look straight ahead, toward the horizon.
- Think of something else. Dwelling on the queasiness tends to make it worse.
- Don't read, draw, color, or do anything else that makes you look down or causes you to feel more nauseated.
- Seat carsick people in the front of the car, or as close as you can manage. Young children who can't sit in front might still do better in the middle seat of a minivan than the back.
- Chew something.
- Close your eyes.
- Nap.
- Open the window a crack, because fresh air seems to help. Sitting next to a window also helps brace your body from extra movement that can aggravate the disagreement between what your body feels and your eyes see. Make sure children in the back have fresh air.
- Stop the car, get out, and walk around until the queasiness goes away.
- If anything in the car smells bad, get rid of it.
- Take an antinausea medication, such as Dramamine.

- Eat ginger, such as ginger cookies or ginger pills. You might even keep a bottle of ginger pills in the glove compartment.
- And just in case, keep a leak-proof bag ready to grab.

When my grandparents took me up a long, windy mountain road to their family cabin at Lake Arrowhead, Grandpa told me to pretend I was driving. I grasped a pretend steering wheel, turning the "wheel" with every bend in the road. The game helped me focus on the road instead of how carsick I was feeling, and I made it to the cabin just fine. —Loralee

When I was a kid, our parents would give us potato chips. The salt seemed to help. Saltine crackers might also be a good option. —Rick

NIGHTTIME

When darkness falls, your children won't be able to see their books and toys. Here are some ways to keep them enjoying themselves:

- Save "dinner" or final snacks for when it's really dark.
- Pass out headlamps or book lights to allow them to keep reading or playing (warn them that if their lights distract the driver, the lights must go off).
- Pass out electronics with light-up screens.
- Turn on some music for singing.
- Turn on a movie.
- Turn on some quiet music to lull them to sleep—just don't put the driver to sleep!

If you want your children to sleep in the car, you may want to try a bedtime routine. If your family has a nightly ritual, such as talking about the day, reading a bedtime story, or saying prayers, do as much as you can in the car. It may help calm your children down and get them ready to go to sleep.

FAMILY TALK TIME

When everybody's jammed into a tiny space in the car, you might think you're too close for comfort. But you can turn this closeness into an advantage. With no phones ringing, laundry to wash, or work to rush off to, you have uninterrupted time to concentrate on your children.

Take advantage of this time to really talk to your children, if you can get them to open up. Ask about their school, their sports, their friends, their favorite books and TV shows, or their dreams for the future. Listen closely to what they tell you and try not to interrupt or interject. Interview them about their lives and invite them to interview you. You might be astonished at what you learn.

Don't ignore your spouse, either. If the kids fall asleep, turn off the audio and talk.

When we're at home, we're always getting distracted by kids, work, chores, and everything else. Our best conversations about growing up, the ins and outs of my husband's work, or our future plans happen when we're driving together.
—Loralee

FRIENDS AND RELATIVES

In areas with good cell phone coverage, you might enjoy getting on the phone and catching up with relatives or letting your children talk to family members. Your immediate family will appreciate hearing occasional status updates so that everybody knows where you are and how you're doing.

Although it's fun to catch up with distant friends and relatives, don't let it detract from family time. Some travelers choose to avoid distractions like e-mail, Facebook, or texting and concentrate on spending time with family instead.

CHAPTER NINE

Stopping for Breaks

On one drive to Utah, we found a lovely state park in Oregon that's now one of our favorite places to take a travel break. We use the bathroom, play tag on the grass, wade in the river, and search for frogs. We can even read signs about the Oregon Trail. We're always refreshed by the beauty and fresh air, which helps us face the rest of the long trip. —Loralee

You finally got everybody in the car. Now you have to stop, whether for gas, bathroom breaks, or food. Are you going to take a fast break or take some time to enjoy being out of the car? What essentials do you need to take care of? And how can you get everybody out of the car and back in without losing too much time?

STOPPING FOR GAS

Watch the gas gauge as you drive and try to fill your tank before you're down to a quarter of a tank. Don't get too close to empty—the adrenaline rush you'll get watching for gas stations as the needle drops isn't worth it! Besides, you'll want to stop every few hours to stretch legs and use the bathroom; you may as well gas up when you do.

If you're driving through isolated areas, such as the Southwest, gas stations may be few and far between. Learn your route before you go so that you'll know where the towns and gas stations are, and don't pass up your chance to gas up if you suspect it'll be miles before the next town.

When we drove to Banff, I was surprised by two things. One was how beautiful it was; the mountain scenery took my breath away. The other was how long we had to drive between breaks, because the road we were on had hardly any off-ramps with services. So we had to plan our breaks carefully to make sure we didn't run out of gas in the middle of nowhere. —Elaine

LONG STOPS VS. SHORT STOPS

Will you fill up near the freeway or in town? Stations near the freeway usually have higher prices, but driving into town to look for something cheaper could burn up time without saving you much money. (For instance, if you drive to find a station where gas is four cents cheaper than at the freeway and you put twenty gallons in your tank, you've only saved eighty cents.) You'll need to decide which is more important: your time or your money.

Sometimes it's fun to drive through an unfamiliar town and read signs or admire buildings. If it's mealtime, you might want to stop at a grocery store or try a local restaurant (check Yelp.com or Tripadvisor.com for recommendations).

On the other hand, you might rather keep traveling so that you can reach your destination quickly. In that case, fuel up at the nearest gas station. Stations just off the freeway are more likely to have resources for travelers, such as attached dining, convenience stores, clean rest rooms, maps, and tourist information, than in-town facilities. Truck stops tend to have the most resources.

GAS STATION BREAKS

Treat the gas stop as a relaxed but efficient version of a NASCAR pit stop. Take care of all the tasks you can't do while you're driving. Wash windows, straighten and reorganize around the feet and on seats, get out snacks, and fill water bottles. (Most gas stations will let you refill water bottles for free.) Throw away trash, drink bottles, and scraps. Empty out your trash bag or box, or throw the whole thing away and set up a replacement trash container. Make sure you can access whatever you might need during the next stretch. If the driver is tired, allow time for a short catnap or a short brisk walk, or restock on eye-opening beverages. If you have a top carrier, check it.

Kids need attention, too. Make sure everyone goes to the bathroom and gets a chance to stretch their legs. If your kids are old enough, let them pump the gas and help wash the windows. They enjoy it, and it's a good learning experience.

STOPPING AT REST STOPS

When you stop at a rest stop, send all the children to the bathroom, even if somebody says, "I don't need to go." Otherwise, you may spend all day leapfrogging from one rest stop to the next as one child after another finally speaks up.

Take advantage of open spaces at rest stops to let your children run around. You might also want to pull out snacks or even a picnic.

GET MOVING

After riding in a car for hours, kids need to move around. So do the grownups. When you get out of the car, get everybody moving fast. Invent races, like running to the nearest tree and back again. Hold "Olympic" events, like backwards-walking races. Play tag or follow-the-leader and chase your kids around for a while. They'll give you a workout! If you have more time, start a game of whiffle ball or Frisbee. If it's dark, try flashlight tag.

> We always carried a whiffle ball and bat as we drove across the country. Then we'd make sure to play an inning or two in each state. —Michele

Even if you're in a small place like a gas station, you can get kids moving. Have them jump up and down or make up dance moves. They can also run on the sidewalk outside or do jumping jacks.

STOPPING TO SIGHTSEE

If you know your kids are going to need time out of the car, you may want to schedule some sightseeing stops. Check the map for historical sites, local museums, state parks, national landmarks, or small towns to explore. You can get everybody out of the car, explore someplace new and exciting, and then be back on your way.

Your kids want to run, chase each other, and yell, but make sure their activities suit their surroundings. At parks and playgrounds, your kids will love running, playing, and working out excess energy. But if they run through crowds or public places, pushing through people and yelling, they might upset bystanders or even knock people over. Teach your children to be aware of their environment and to be courteous to those around them.

SIGHTSEEING AT BREAKS

Even impromptu stops offer new things to see and learn. Many rest stops have landscapes worth exploring or signs to help you learn about the area and its history. If you stop at state parks or national landmarks, you might find hiking trails, historical sites you've never heard of, or scenery you never imagined.

> *On one drive to Colorado, our four-year-old started yelling for a bathroom. We pulled off onto a dirt road and found a hiking trailhead. While my husband took care of our daughter, I read a historic sign. To my amazement, the sign told the story of a train accident that had happened there a hundred years before: train engineers saw a burning bridge ahead, pulled the brakes, and jumped off the train, slowing the train enough to save the oblivious passengers still on board. We never would have learned anything about it if we hadn't had to stop. —Loralee*

DENTS AND DINGS

When you stop for a break, you may notice new chips from highway gravel or new rock chips in the windshield. In crowded parking lots, you might get new dents as careless drivers bang their doors into yours. When you're traveling, it's hard to avoid car damage. Expect it to happen and keep driving.

I always welcome the first dent—it's over, and I don't have to stress anymore about keeping my car pristine. And if our car did not look fresh off the assembly line (a family car seldom does), I was less worried about it getting stolen. —Rick

CHAPTER TEN

Sightseeing

We'd been avoiding Disneyland for years, since the price was so high and there were so many ways to entertain children without rides. But when our in-laws planned a Disneyland trip at the same time we were going to California, we decided we'd do it. When the gates opened, we rushed to our first ride: Pinocchio. Only then did I realize that my children's lack of amusement park experience might be a problem: as the car lurched forward, our young daughter started screaming at the top of her lungs. After four rides ended in tearstains and hysteria, I wondered if we were about to spend our hundred-dollar day in our hotel room. Luckily, a ride on the carousel settled my daughter down, and we were able to enjoy the magic of Disneyland. —Loralee

You've finally arrived at your destination. What's the best way to enjoy your visit?

VISITING ATTRACTIONS

When you're visiting attractions like amusement parks, museums, or zoos, a little preparation will make your visit much more enjoyable—and maybe even cheaper!

Admission Discounts

It never hurts to see if there's a way your family can get a discount on entrance fees.

- Check ahead to see if cheaper tickets are offered online or through a store like Costco. For instance, Costco sells Disneyland tickets at a discount.
- Check for AAA, CAA, or military discounts, if you qualify. (AAA and CAA discounts are available at many attractions and restaurants.)
- Check memberships. Buying a family membership might pay for itself if you visit the attraction twice. A membership to a zoo or museum in your hometown might get you free or discounted admission into partner organizations.
- See if your destination offers any sort of pass for multiple attractions. In many cities, you can buy a pass that gets you into the city's top spots, and it's cheaper than paying for each separately.

Food

Tourist attractions invariably charge more for food than you want to pay. Often, it's not even food you want to feed your kids! If you're concerned about hungry children, see what snacks you can pack along. You might be able to bring a full meal with sandwiches and drinks, or you might be able to stuff a bag of crackers, dried fruit, or nuts into your purse to stave off hunger pangs until you can feed your children a real meal.

Be careful with any snacks you pack. You don't want your children spilling snacks or drinks in museums, and you don't want to leave your snacks (or other possessions) unattended.

When I visited the Seattle zoo, I packed a bag of Goldfish crackers in the stroller. After I left the stroller outside of one exhibit, I found that a crow had torn open my bag of crackers and gobbled them up. All that was left was a pile of tiny crumbs. —Loralee

You should also check ahead to see whether food is allowed. If you pack it up and find you can't bring it, you may have to abandon your plans to visit the attraction, or throw the food away.

When I visited Chicago with family members, we decided to visit the art museum. On the way, we stopped for Chicago's signature caramel corn and bought huge bags to take home as gifts. But the museum wouldn't let us take the caramel corn inside or check it at the door, so my sister had to stay outside with all the popcorn. —Loralee

You can often find a restaurant or fast-food place outside the attraction with far cheaper prices for food. Just consider whether the money you save will be worth the lost time.

Supplies

Make sure you have everything you need for your visit, such as camera gear, jackets, or baby supplies. You'll also need a way to pack and carry everything around, such as a backpack, a shoulder bag, or a stroller.

We thought we were all ready for Disneyland. We'd been prepped on where to go first (Fantasyland) and which app to download to check line times (Mousewait). We'd also packed our camera, snacks, baby wipes, and extra diapers. But all that preparation wasn't enough—after a series of messy diapers depleted our diaper supplies, it took me an hour of running around Disneyland with a toddler to buy replacements! —Loralee

KEEPING TRACK OF EVERYTHING

Children

When you're traveling, it's easy to lose track of your children. Consider dressing your children in bright colors or in matching outfits so that you can easily spot them in a crowd. Make sure each child is assigned to an adult so that nobody wanders off when each parent thinks the other is in charge. If you trade children, make sure both adults know about the switch so that one child doesn't follow Dad and get lost because Dad doesn't realize he or she is there.

When we're out as a family, instead of my husband and me generally watching the kids, each of us pays particular attention to specific children. If either of us wants to change which children we are watching, we say "positive handoff," and the other parent acknowledges the handoff. That way, we make sure we both know which parent is watching which children. —Colette

Your children should also carry your contact information. Make sure older children have memorized your phone numbers. You might also want to give them a little bit of cash in case of emergencies. For younger children, prepare ID cards, name bracelets, labels for clothing, contact information written inside their shoes, or whatever else you can think of.

As we approached Disneyland, where a huge crowd of people were milling at the gates, I realized how easy it would be to lose track of our children, who didn't have ID cards or shoe labels or anything. So I rushed into a store, borrowed a ballpoint pen, and wrote our cell phone numbers on their arms. —Loralee

Consider making a family plan in case you get separated or in case you're going to let older children explore on their own. If children get lost, whom should they approach for help, and what should they tell them? If you get separated or if you split up, where would be a good place to meet up? (Make sure it's an easy place to find.) If your children need to check back with you periodically, when and where should they go?

Car

When you park, pay close attention to where you've parked and where you go from there, so that you can easily retrace your steps. You might even use your smartphone to take a picture of your parking space or nearby location signs. If you have a top carrier (or two) on the car, it'll really stand out in a crowded parking lot!

Valuables

While it's helpful to carry some cash, carry only what you'll need during the day. Try using a credit card instead. Stolen credit cards can be replaced, but stolen cash is gone forever. If you're staying in a secure location, like a good hotel room or a friend's house, you can leave extra cash, credit cards, or valuables in your room, instead of in your purse, pocket, or car.

Be careful where you carry valuables. Don't carry them in a place that's easily accessible to pickpockets, such as a backpack, an over-the-shoulder purse, or a back pocket. Front pockets or money pouches are more secure.

ENJOYING NEW CITIES

Once you've arrived at your destination, keep your eyes open for opportunities. Check local flyers, newspapers, or ads for local events that you might not otherwise learn about. You'll find concerts, events, and other fun occasions that will really add to your trip.

> *When we were in Florida, I read in the events section of a local newspaper that humorist Dave Barry would be speaking and signing at a bookstore in South Miami. We hopped in the car, took a beautiful drive down the coast, stopped at a couple of beaches, and topped the day off listening to and meeting one of my favorite authors. —Rick*

One way to experience new places is to try the food. Be adventurous when you order, or try at least one new thing when you order your usual favorites. Who knows—your family might fall in love with poutine, ketchup chips, hush puppies, deep-fried cheese curds, clam cakes, carnitas, Fritos pie, spaghetti pizza, or alligator sausage!

Enjoy and embrace the differences you find in new places. It's all part of the journey.

ENCOURAGING RELUCTANT CHILDREN

When you choose activities for the parents to enjoy, children might lose interest quickly. If you can keep them interested and happy, you'll all have a better visit.

General Tips

Are your children fussing for a reason? Are they overtired, hungry, or thirsty? Do they need to run around and make noise? If you can pinpoint their problems, you can try to solve them. Fussy children might calm down if you stop for lunch, for a drink, or for a few minutes outside where they can run around.

Museums

Even young children can enjoy museum displays, if you help them. Talk to them in ways they can understand. If you're admiring a Monet water lily painting, you might say something like "Look at those flowers floating in the water! What color are the flowers? Would you like to swim in that pond?" In a history museum, you might explain what you're looking at and turn the history into an exciting story or something your children can relate to. Your children might not leave with a complete understanding of impressionism or American history, but if you can help them admire an exhibit or learn something new, you've succeeded.

> We joined an art museum when our children were four and two years old. At the Gates of Paradise exhibit, we talked about the Bible stories portrayed in the golden panels. At an exhibit of Roman artifacts, I showed my two-year-old all the animals I could find, such as sacrificial bulls and a lamp shaped like a bird. It wasn't a very scholarly discussion, but he was fascinated, and it gave me the time to admire the artwork and quickly read signs. Both children loved it so much that they begged to go to the museum again and again! —Loralee

Children might also enjoy using museum audio guides and computers, watching videos, jumping on colored floor tiles, playing with smartphones, reading their own picture books, or playing with toys you've brought in. If they can do these things without distracting patrons, causing a disruption, damaging anything, or alerting the security guards, let them! Any minute you can distract your children is an extra minute you can enjoy the museum for yourself.

Many museums have children's activity areas. If you don't mind taking extra time, stop there for a break so children can play or regroup. This might be a good opportunity to talk about what you see in the museum without distracting other patrons with loud conversation.

Be mindful of children in museums and keep your children close. You want them to enjoy the experience, not ruin it for somebody else. Help them be quiet and respectful so that you don't bother other patrons. Keep them a safe distance away from the artwork, and if they get too loud and wiggly, take them out for a break.

Hiking

In many national parks, the best way to see the sights is to hike to them. How can you manage this with small children?

First, learn about what you can see inside the park and how to see it. You might decide that what you can see from the car is good enough or find viewpoints you can drive to even if you can't get as close as you would on a hiking trail.

If you do decide to take your children on hiking trails, try different ways to encourage them along.

- See if you can take a stroller on the trail or carry infants in a baby pack.
- Point out interesting things as you go. Even when you can't see major sites, you can talk about the colors of

flowers, the shapes of rocks, wild birds and animals, or how long it might take to get to the next bend.

- Challenge your children to races, such as who can reach the next bend in the trail. Many children will perk up with a challenge.
- Carry plenty of water and stop for breaks when necessary.
- If your children have had enough, turn back. You've seen wonderful things already, and whatever's at the end of the trail will still be there next time you come.

When we're hiking at places like the Grand Canyon and the kids get tired, we chant the family mantra: "We're the Shirks! We're one year older, and we're one year stronger!" Nobody complains after hearing the mantra. Instead, they realize they're older and stronger, and they keep going. —Rachel

Parents' Night Out

If there's a grownup event you want to attend, you might be able to find a way. Some theater events offer child care or can refer you to a trustworthy child care service. Others have family seats or a family box where you and your children can watch the event without distracting other patrons. Some resorts or tourist attractions have children's events or classes.

If you're staying with friends or family, ask if you can trade babysitting or if they can recommend a babysitter. You could even hire a babysitter, and then take your hosts out to dinner to thank them for their generosity.

MAKING MEMORIES

You want your vacation to be a memorable experience. Don't rely on your memory! Help your memory along by taking photos and videos, blogging as you go, writing in your journal, keeping a scrapbook, or saving souvenirs. But beware of spending so much time behind the camera that you forget to look at what you came to see.

Photos

With digital cameras, film is free. You can take as many photos as you want, so don't hold back. Think about what kind of pictures you'll want later—pictures of the attraction, pictures of your children, or family pictures all together.

Souvenirs

What kinds of souvenirs will you buy on your trip? Do you like to buy mugs, posters, or silver spoons? Do your children really need more T-shirts or stuffed animals? Think ahead about the kinds of souvenirs you want or set a souvenir budget so that you don't splurge on things you'll soon tire of.

If you're buying souvenirs for your children, tell them ahead of time what you're willing to buy. You might also give each of them money they can spend on their own, or invite them to bring their own money for purchases.

Many national parks and tourist attractions are surrounded by shops that sell the same kinds of souvenirs at cheaper prices, so you don't have to splurge. Thrift stores have the lowest prices of all, and you never know what interesting souvenirs you might find.

If you're traveling abroad, look for things that are different from what you have back home. Even a grocery store turns up great souvenirs. For instance, Cadbury bars in the US are limited to various chocolate bars made by Hershey, but in Canada you can find exotic Cadbury treats such as Crunchie bars, Sweet Marie bars, or Wunderbars.

Our kids always get Kinder Surprise Eggs when we visit Canada. They love eating the chocolate eggs and finding the toys inside. But we have to eat the eggs before we come home, because it's illegal to bring them into the US! —Colette

Foreign money also makes a great souvenir. Not only is it beautiful but it might be very different from what's at home. For instance, Americans use pennies but Canadians don't (they now round to the nearest nickel), and Americans use one-dollar bills while Canadians use one-dollar coins.

When my nephew visited a museum in Victoria, BC, his father gave him Canadian money to buy something. My nephew thought it was so cool that he kept the money for a souvenir and didn't buy anything. —Loralee

Some ideas for family souvenirs:

- Postcards (the pictures are often better than any photos you can take)
- T-shirts or hats that you can continue to wear
- Christmas ornaments
- Books or activity books about what you've seen, to help your children remember
- Lotions, lip balms, or treats: you can use them and enjoy memories of your trip and then discard them when they're used up
- Toys or activities that children can play with on the long car ride home, even if they probably won't use them afterwards

WHEN TO KEEP GOING AND WHEN TO STOP

Traveling leads to long days. Sometimes it's tempting to visit just one more museum, exhibit, or ride, even when your children are falling apart. Other times, you might get so frustrated by traveling with children that you'd rather spend the rest of your vacation in your hotel.

Sightseeing with children is a delicate balance. On the one hand, you've spent a lot of time and money to get where you are, and you don't want to waste either. On the other hand, your children probably can't handle as much as you can. If your children get too bored, exhausted, or miserable without proper attention and rest, they'll fall apart.

Make sure your children get what they need to stay happy and healthy through your whole trip, whether it's midday naps, frequent snacks, or early bedtimes. You might also enjoy your experience more if you take breaks from rushing around.

On the other hand, if your kids can handle it, don't turn down a chance to see something new. It may turn out to be the highlight of your trip.

After a trip to Glacier National Park, we drove late into the night to visit grandparents. When they suggested we go on a hike the next morning, I just wanted to sleep! But my husband wanted to go, so we all went. When we finally made it to the top, we were surrounded by golden wheat fields below, crisscrossed with the trails of combine harvesters. We'd never seen anything like it, and I was so glad I went! —Loralee

CHAPTER ELEVEN

Back Home

"No man needs a vacation so much as the man who has just had one." —*Elbert Hubbard*

Your vacation is almost over. You've seen the sights, taken thousands of photos, and worn everybody out. Now you're heading home. But don't forget about your trip too soon—there's still a lot to do!

RETURNING HOME

How can you help everybody enjoy the return trip? Some families choose a different road back for variety, some families stop for more sightseeing on the way home, and some families travel directly home to keep the return trip fast.

When we drove along the Icefields Parkway linking Banff and Jasper, I was amazed by the beautiful glaciered mountains, tree-lined valleys, and clear, blue lakes. When we returned, we tried to find an alternate route home so we could see some different sights, but there wasn't one. As we drove back along the same road, the scenery looked completely different. Traveling the opposite direction was like going on a brand-new road, and it was just as beautiful. —Elaine

Using up Currency

If you've been traveling in a foreign country, you probably have some extra local currency. If you decide to spend it before you cross the border, consider buying something you'll need anyway, such as snacks or treats for the drive back home. Otherwise, you can exchange bills at a currency exchange or at a bank back home, but you will be charged a small fee. (You usually can't exchange coins.) You might also want to keep your extra money for your next trip across the border.

Whenever my father crossed a border, he would stop at a gas station and spend his remaining local currency on gasoline. This allowed him to use up every last penny. —Elaine

BEFORE YOU ARRIVE

As you're driving home, call ahead to see if somebody at home would be willing to go to your house and get it ready for you. Ask them to turn on porch lights if yours aren't automatic, and to turn on the heat or air conditioning a few hours before you arrive. This will make your home a much more welcoming place.

WHEN YOU GET THERE

When you arrive home, your first priority is to take care of your kids. Get them out of the car for snacks, a meal, playtime, or whatever they need. If it's late, put them to bed right away.

After that, start cleaning up. It's not very fun, but it's easier to do sooner than later.

Unpacking the Car

Bring in the luggage, especially your valuables and electronics. The more you can unload from your car when you arrive home, the less you'll have to do later. Remember, unpacking is part of the trip.

Whenever we went on car trips when I was a kid, my dad always had us unpack the car as soon as we rolled into the driveway. We'd all stagger in with loads of luggage until the car was completely unpacked. Now when we arrive home from vacation, my husband is usually wiped out from driving the entire trip, so unpacking is my job. I haul in all the cameras, computers, electronics, and other valuables. I bring in the food in case some of it needs to be refrigerated or in case we need something to snack on as we work on unpacking. I also bring in the suitcases because we end up needing pajamas or toothbrushes as we get children ready for bed. I might leave sleeping bags or dirty laundry in the car, but I know that if I leave it too long, I'll forget and drive it around forever. It always feels great to get the car unpacked.
—Loralee

Cleaning Out the Car

If you're like most families, you'll probably jump back into your hectic schedule as soon as you're home. Clean out your car right away if you can, because it'll soon fill up with all the detritus from your normal schedule.

- Bring in all the luggage and travel supplies.
- Go through your car and throw out trash. If you don't have time to sort everything right away, bring

everything from the car inside and decide later what to do with it. But don't wait very long—it's too easy to leave a box of junk on your floor for months.

- Vacuum your seats and floor. You'll be surprised (and horrified) by the crumbs or messes your children might have spilled in the back seats!

Unpacking Your Suitcases

If you can start unpacking right away, you'll make your life much easier. You'll be able to start washing dirty laundry, you'll be able to find the things that were packed away, and you'll be able to clear suitcase clutter off of your floor.

Ask older children to unpack their own suitcases. If you help them learn where things are stored, such as the suitcases or travel supplies, they'll be able to put things away and minimize mess.

> Once when I was packing for a trip, I searched for my travel toothbrush but couldn't find it anywhere. In desperation, I packed my good toothbrush instead. Only when I returned home did I notice a backpack in my bedroom, still holding all the gear I'd used for a camping trip the previous month. My travel toothbrush was inside. —Loralee

Cleaning and Restocking

If you keep a standard set of travel supplies, replace what you used on your trip, such as soap, shampoo, razors, or toothpaste. You'll also want to restock whatever emergency supplies you may have used in your car, such as food or first aid items.

> After a trip, I wash toothbrushes in the dishwasher, let them dry, and put them in clean baggies labeled with each

*traveler's name. I also refill my travel shampoo bottle with my
regular conditioning shampoo so that I never have to wash
with hotel shampoo that turns my hair into dandelion fluff.*
—Loralee

MAKING MEMORIES

You worked so hard to take your family on vacation and (hopefully) had lots of great experiences. Don't let those memories fade away. You can keep your trip alive and continue to enjoy it long after your journey has ended.

- Blog about your travels or post photos on Facebook.
- Share your photos with online albums.
- Make a digital photo book with all your favorite memories.
- Make extra copies of photos, or even a trip album, for your children.
- Put photos, tickets, brochures, maps, and other memorabilia in a scrapbook.
- Use a picture from your trip for your family Christmas card.
- Talk about your trip with your children, with comments like "Look, there's a picture of the Grand Canyon! We were there just last month!" or "Remember when we went to the San Francisco Zoo? What animals did you like?"

*After we took a major trip with our four-year-old daughter,
we read books about where we'd been, made a scrapbook to
look at, and talked about the trip often. Six years later, my
daughter still has vivid memories of the buildings we explored
and the museums we visited.* —Loralee

RELIVING VACATION HIGHLIGHTS

Is there anything you enjoyed on your trip that you can do at home? If your family enjoyed doing puzzles, playing games, going on walks together, or other activities, do them again when you're home. If you enjoyed sightseeing, hiking outdoors, going to zoos, or other activities, see what your own area has to offer and go try it out.

> *Whenever we travel, I resolve to remember our adventures and continue them at home. I bring home things like Maine blueberry jam to eat together, decide to have family board game nights as we did in our beach cabin, or remind myself that if we've enjoyed our vacation fireplace, we can light a fire in our own fireplace. But as we get sucked back into the demands of our busy family schedule, all my resolutions get forgotten, the jam sits in the cupboard, and the games gather dust on the shelf. It's too easy to neglect quiet family time—until the next time we go on vacation. —Loralee*

GETTING READY FOR NEXT TIME

Now that you've conquered one family trip, think about where else you'd like to take your family. If you drove east, why not go west? If you visited mountains, why not drive to the coast? If you hiked through forests, what about visiting grasslands?

We live in on a beautiful continent, with more to explore and enjoy than you could visit in a thousand years of road trips. No matter how much you travel, you can always find more cities to explore, more hikes to attempt, more museums to visit, more history to learn, more foods to taste, and more highways to drive. So watch for new ideas, think up new adventures, and get ready for your next road trip!

Family Bios

ADAM AND DANIELLE T.

Adam and Danielle live in Utah with their five children.

- Favorite car activity: Buy little toys and things ahead of time. Hand them out every hour so the kids always have something new.

ERIK AND BRITNEY BASSETT

Erik and Britney currently reside in the beautiful mountain town of Flagstaff, Arizona, and love being outside as a family. They have become professional short-road-trippers as their family lives 2.5 hours away and they make the drive frequently.

- Kids' ages: 4, 2
- Favorite car activity: special snacks for the car (Mom likes anything that takes a long time to eat!), craft activities (like coloring or doing stamps), and books on tape in the car.

JAMES AND AMANDA G.

My introduction to road tripping was driving from Utah to Texas for a family move. Picture six children, two adults and a dog in a Chevy station wagon. I'm sure my parents viewed the trip with trepidation, but I remember it fondly. James and I now drive from Seattle to California with our two girls.

- Favorite car activities: We stay happy in the car with sticker books, games, and drawing supplies.
- Favorite car snack: Pringles and breakfast bars

JAMES AND COLETTE F.

We're both from Canada, but moved to Washington. We regularly take our four boys on road trips to Alberta to see family.

- Kids' ages: 10, 8, 5, 2
- Favorite car snack: Goldfish

- Favorite car activity: ABC game, where you look at signs, license plates, etc. to find all the letters of the alphabet
- Favorite road trip: Driving from Seattle to the Redwoods for a family reunion. We were able to take more time, so we weren't as stressed. At one point we stopped at the ocean and James got too close to the waves, so he got wet!

JASON AND RACHEL SHIRK

We both grew up taking family road trips, but they were usually to the same place every year, and our parents planned out the quickest, most stress-free routes to get there. We decided that our road trips would always be full of adventure. The final destination is often the same, but how we get there changes with every trip.

- Kids' ages: 17, 12, 10, 8
- Favorite car snack: going to Sonic Drive-thru for tater tots
- Favorite car activity: following along on our own maps
- Favorite road trip: All of them. We never see the same thing twice!

JIM AND CHERYL L.

Jim and Cheryl live in a small town in Utah. When their seven children were growing up, they took the kids to Yellowstone, Arizona, Missouri, Denver, Canada, Wyoming, and South Dakota.

- Favorite car snack: Ding Dongs, cans of Vienna sausages, stopping at the gas station to let kids choose some kind of candy because they never had candy at home (this also kept kids occupied with their favorite treat)
- Favorite car activity: Get off the beaten track, follow a back road, and go for a hike or wade in a crick or find something surprising. Recently when we pulled off in a forest in Oregon, we found markers for the original Oregon Trail.
- Favorite road trip: On one road trip the campgrounds were all full so we threw out our sleeping bags in a state park, and in the morning the sprinklers came on. Or there was one night

we slept out in a pasture and in the morning we woke up to a big old bull standing over us—we got out of there in a hurry! Or there was that time we stopped for the night on the way to Arizona and slept on a blanket on soft, warm desert sand, and in the morning Jim woke up and said "Don't move!" because there was a rattlesnake right by our heads, so he counted to three and we ran away and didn't get bit. Or there was the time we camped outside Yellowstone and a bear came into camp (that's what you get when you throw down your sleeping bag just any old place). Or when we wanted to camp in Yellowstone but there was no camping allowed, so we had to use our gas money for a hotel and our food money for gas. . . . Wait, when you said "favorite," you meant "memorable," right?

JONATHAN AND KATHRYN STAPLEY

Jonathan and Kathryn live in Washington, but they take a long car trip at least once a year.

- Kids' ages: 12, 10, 2, 5 months
- Favorite car snack: Let each kid pick their favorite snack—they usually get something they never have at home.
- Favorite car activity:
  - Mom: book on CD
  - Dad: music from his own road trip mix CD, which the kids learn to like
  - Kids: video games
  - They also plan to try a friend's system of rotating between one hour of music, one hour of story, one hour of movie, and one hour of silence.
- Favorite road trip: Yellowstone

JOSH AND LESLIE L.

Josh says he suffers from one of the few known cases of carcolepsy, a disease that closely resembles narcolepsy but only manifests in the car. Leslie does most of the driving (I know, how modern!)

for her sanity and the family safety. The children have come to terms with long haul road trips and only really start to bicker after the first fifteen minutes. The secret to long road trips is to provide ample spacing between children (one seat minimum) and plenty of Diet Pepsi and snacks. Letting the kids each pick a treat at the gas station stops is worth the cost (both in dollars and rotten teeth) by providing brief spells of mouth-filled peace.

- Kids' ages: 11, 8, and 5
- Favorite car snack:
  - Josh: Jerky (low calorie and delicious)
  - Leslie: Diet Pepsi
  - Caleb: Sour Patch Watermelons
  - Sydney: Crackers
  - Mylee: Chips
- Favorite car activity: Reading, drawing, music, video games, and movies
- Favorite road trip: Driving from Utah to Michigan and back around the Michigan Upper Peninsula

KENDRA AND PAUL PETERSON

The whole family has only been on one road trip together, a six-hour round-trip to Portland. Everyone survived. But Kendra and her two daughters can regularly be seen in the Seattle area pulled over at the park or library eating packed lunches from home. It's like a road trip every day!

You can find Kendra channeling her creativity into making fun waste-free bento lunches on her blog, Biting the Hand That Feeds You, at http://www.bitingthehandthatfeedsyou.net

- Kids' ages: 5, almost 2
- Favorite car snack: Anything crunchy: popcorn, nuts, apples, corn chips, etc.
- Favorite car activity: singing along to the radio without being shushed by those in the back seat (their favorite activity is looking at books).

KENT AND ELAINE BASSETT

Kent and Elaine raised five children in the Seattle area. They often took the kids to visit family in Eastern Washington, California, and Utah.

- Favorite car snack: red licorice for driver, apples for kids
- Favorite car activity: books on tape and general knowledge questions like asking kids to name twenty national parks
- Favorite road trip: Yellowstone

LARAMIE AND LORALEE LEAVITT

We drive from Seattle to Utah at least twice a year to see family, and we often take a detour on the way out or back.

- Kids' ages: 10, 8, 5, newborn
- Favorite car snack: sliced apples for everyone, Coke Zero and dark chocolate Schoolboy cookies for the driver only!
- Favorite car activity: audiobooks, singing, reading, Crayola Color Wonder
- Favorite road trip: The one where we drove to Utah, then to Arizona via Las Angeles to see grandparents. Or the one to California when we only had two days' notice. Or the one where we added Mt. Rushmore onto a trip to Denver. Hmm . . .

MARK W.

Mark lives in Canada and works in the book business.

- Favorite car snack: Tim Horton's
- Favorite road trip: Toronto to Halifax

MICHAEL COREY

Originally from Berkeley, California, I've lived in Alaska, Colorado, Massachusetts, and Washington. I've driven across the US six times and the Alaska Highway twice.

- Kids' ages: 16, 14
- Favorite car snack: My car snacks have changed with my health focus but sandwiches still keep people happy.

- Favorite car activity: I used to tell Peter Rhinoceros stories when the boys were little. Sometimes we used to play the alphabet game, where you look for each letter of the alphabet on a sign somewhere (in order). Telling stories with one sentence per person is fun—the idea is to make it so crazy that the next person has a challenge pulling it together. Now my boys are at the age of the smart phone, so car trips are not very interactive.
- Favorite road trip: I love trips to the San Juans and up in the Georgia Strait.

MICHELE AND CHRISTOPHER ROBBINS

Christopher and I are blessed with nine wonderful children, a dog, and a Suburban to smash into for road trips and around-town rambles. When we are brave enough to load all the kids and the dog in the car, we escape to the mountains to camp, hike, climb, and enjoy family time.

- Kids' ages: 21, 18, 16, 14, 12, 9, 6, 3, and 3
- Favorite car snack: We all like different things so I grab a variety of healthy and totally not healthy foods—apples, carrots, crackers, hard candies, and gum. Brownies also go over very well—they go over the kids clothes, the car upholstery, and the floor. We take them anyway, Yum.
- Favorite car activity: Guess the animal. This keeps the kids studying up and learning new species to try to stump their sibling and, yes, their parents as well.
- Favorite road trip: Dinosaur Monument, Utah

MIKE AND SUSAN COLLIER

We are from Washington, but we moved to Utah. We like movies, music, and goofing around with our girls. We took a family road trip to Arizona a couple years back thru Vegas and we usually visit Washington every other year. When we do, we leave Utah at 4 pm and drive all night. Mike's the driver until about 2 am, when we're almost to Oregon. I wake up and finish the drive, and we make it to his parents' house right in time for breakfast, then we both take a nap while the kids have fun with Grandma, Grandpa, and uncles. The next trip we will be taking should be next year, to Brazil—not a road trip, but an adventure.

- Kids' ages: 13, 11, 10-year-old twins
- Favorite car snack: Wheat thins, candy for Mike, food from 72 hour kits, McDonalds for food and restroom break (if there aren't any other options)

RICK AND ANN WALTON

Rick and Ann have driven on many long trips with their five children, including from Utah to New York and Florida. Rick always takes a car top carrier for extra space, zip bags for organizing, and CDs of the family's favorite storytellers.

RAISSA AND ANDY SCHNEIDER

We live in the Seattle area, and we take our two girls on a lot of road trips to visit family in Eastern Washington (Wenatchee). We pretty much just like to do anything together.

- Kids' ages: 4 and 7
- Favorite car snack: Lara bars, fruit leather, or anything that doesn't make crumbs
- Favorite car activity: I Spy or some game with car colors or something that requires observation skills and everybody can play
- Favorite road trip: Driving to Wenatchee to see family

SPENCER AND EMILY FUGAL

Spencer and I grew up mostly in Utah. Our family has lived in the Seattle area for about eight years. We love playing outside (hiking, camping, biking, swimming, etc.). Our road trips have mostly been back home to Utah to visit family. We have also taken a couple of road trips to California on vacations. We often take road trips camping to various places, mostly in Washington and Utah.

- Kids' ages: 11, 9, 6, 3
- Favorite car snack: a variety of fresh veggies (carrots, cauliflower, cucumbers, etc.).
- Favorite car activity: listening to audio books together, usually kids fiction.
- Favorite road trip: going to Utah to see our family (grandparents, cousins, aunts and uncles).

TONY AND AMANDA M.

Between the two of them, Tony and Amanda have lived about everywhere in the world except for Antarctica and Oklahoma. They love to take their kids traveling.

- Kids' ages: 14, 10, 8
- Favorite car snack: Our favorite part of road trips is the food. It's a treat to eat out even if it is at a gas station! With the kids being older we now look for snacks and foods that are new and may be unique to the area we are traveling.

About the Authors

A popular freelance writer for both parents and children, Loralee Leavitt has been featured in *Family Fun*, *Parents*, *Mothering*, *ParentMap*, *Highlights*, and *Cricket*. She is also the author of *Candy Experiments*, a book of spectacular science experiments with candy. An experienced road-tripper, Loralee Leavitt loves to listen to audiobooks, take photos, and sing with her children on long family drives.

Rick Walton first thought of writing for children when his high school English teacher, Joyce Nelson, told him that a story he had written for the class would make a good children's book. But it wasn't until after he had dabbled in business, law, teaching, software design, and almost every other career in the book, that he finally realized that writing for kids was one of the few things that he both enjoyed and was good at. Since then Rick has had over ninety books published. His works include picture books, riddle books, activity books, mini-mysteries, a collection of poetry, and educational and game software. His books have been featured on the IRA Children's Choice list, *Reading Rainbow*, and on *CBS This Morning*. Rick teaches university courses on picture book writing and on the children's book publishing industry.

About Familius

*Welcome to a place where mothers are celebrated, not compared.
Where heart is at the center of our families, and family at the
center of our homes. Where boo boos are still kissed, cake beaters
are still licked, and mistakes are still okay. Welcome to a place
where books—and family—are beautiful. Familius: a book pub-
lisher dedicated to helping families be happy.*

Familius was founded in 2012 with the intent to align the
founders' love of publishing and family with the digital publishing renaissance which occurred simultaneously with the Great
Recession. The founders believe that the traditional family is
the basic unit of society, and that a society is only as strong as
the families that create it. Familius's mission is to help families
be happy. We invite you to participate with us in strengthening
your family by being part of the Familius family. Go to www.
familius.com to subscribe and receive information about our
books, articles, and videos.

Website: www.familius.com
Facebook: www.facebook.com/paterfamilius
Twitter: @familiustalk, @paterfamilius1
Pinterest: www.pinterest.com/familius